Endorsements

"*God's Truth Revealed* speaks to believers and nonbelievers, skeptics and saints. This book is truly for any person who wants a coherent worldview and is willing to ask and seek answers to tough questions. The reflection questions and the "Churchy Words Dictionary" provide a missing link for many Christians seeking to share their testimonies. This is a complete resource with all a leader could need and more, plus a motivating study a participant will enjoy."
—Dr. Betty Hassler, editor, *Open Windows* magazine

"Kathy has very creatively and skillfully crafted a learning experience that explores the essential truths of the Christian faith. She has peppered this study with entertaining and inspirational stories that will motivate the explorer to go deeper with God. I have been waiting for a study that would help seekers explore Christianity for a long time. This is the one we have always needed."
—Gerry Taillon, national ministry leader, Canadian National Baptist Convention

"Get ready for an amazing journey! Kathy's unique approach enables the reader to easily understand biblical truths with the perfect mix of real-life examples that we all can relate to. As you drink up the true understanding of who God is, you become acutely aware of why you are being called to be a part of His amazing kingdom!"
—Sandi Richard, host of *Fixing Dinner* on Food Network Canada

"*God's Truth Revealed* takes a methodical look at who God is and how He can impact our lives. Kathy's real-life stories, based on adults who met Christ as Savior, bring it all together. Grab your neighbors and begin a study next week! It just might make an eternal difference in their lives."
—Diana Davis, author, *Fresh Ideas for Women's Ministry*

GOD'S TRUTH REVEALED

Biblical Foundations
for the Christian Faith

Kathy Howard

NEW HOPE
PUBLISHERS

Birmingham, Alabama

New Hope® Publishers
P. O. Box 12065
Birmingham, AL 35202-2065
www.newhopepublishers.com
New Hope Publishers is a division of WMU®.

Library of Congress Cataloging-in-Publication Data

Howard, Kathy, 1961-
 God's truth revealed : biblical foundations for the Christian faith / Kathy Howard.
    p. cm.
 Includes bibliographical references.
 ISBN-13: 978-1-59669-268-8 (sc)
 ISBN-10: 1-59669-268-5 (sc)
1. Christianity--Essence, genius, nature--Textbooks. 2. Christian life--Biblical teaching--Textbooks. I. Title.
 BT60.H69 2009
 230--dc22

                            2009036308

ISBN-10: 1-59669-268-5
ISBN-13: 978-1-59669-268-8
N094149 • 0310 • 2.5M1

Table of Contents

Foreword by Dr. Mel Blackaby 8

Acknowledgments 11

Introduction 13

Session 1: Where Do I Begin? 15

Session 2: Who Is God? 27

Session 3: Why Am I Here? 37

Session 4: What Went Wrong? 45

Session 5: How Did God Respond? 57

Session 6: How Can I Be Saved? 71

Session 7: How High Is the Price? 83

Session 8: Isn't This Too Good to Be True? 93

Session 9: Is There Hope for My Future? 103

Session 10: What Now? 115

Session 11: How Do I Get to Know God? 127

Session 12: How Do I Follow God? 139

Churchy Words Dictionary 149

Bible Reading Plan for New Christians:
    31 Days to Know God's Plan for Us. 153

Scripture Memory Tips 155

Scripture Memory Plan: The Basics. 159

Scripture Memory Plan: A Section a Month 161

Recommended Resources 163

General Helps for
    Leading a Study for Seekers and New Believers. 167

Leader's Guide. 173

FOREWORD

*J*esus made a significant statement in John 8:32, *"You will know the truth, and the truth will make you free."* In a world that does not always make sense, many people are searching for the truth about life. Deep down in every person is an innate sense that there is something more, something beyond a temporary life on earth. I am convinced that once people hear the truth about God's purpose for their life, they can make an informed choice to respond and experience life as it was meant to be.

The world will give you many different philosophies about life, but you need to listen to Jesus's words about eternal life. The reason that Jesus is the key to understanding truth is that His perspective is much different than anybody else in human history. According to the Bible, Jesus came from eternity into time. He came from heaven down to earth. When He talks about life, He understands where it came from and where it is going.

This study will help you deal with the most important truth in the world. It will give you a biblical understanding concerning the purpose of life — your life in particular. And most important, it will help you know how to have a relationship with God. Could there be anything more worthy of your time and attention?

When it comes to the truth about God, Kathy Howard has embraced a fundamental reality that must be taken into account. God cannot be discovered by the limited capacity of the human mind. If there truly is a God who created all things, He can only be known by revelation. Left to our own devices, a finite human being cannot understand an infinite God; He is beyond us. The Bible says in 1 Corinthians 1:14 that "*the natural man does not receive the things of the Spirit of God, for they are foolishness to him; nor can he know them, because they are spiritually discerned.*" However, God has chosen to reveal Himself to you through the Bible. That is why Kathy has based this study upon the Bible, for it is God's self-revelation to men and women who are searching for Him.

But God has done much more than give us a Bible to read. He also will be your teacher, helping you to understand what the Bible says. His Spirit will communicate with your spirit, allowing you to understand spiritual truth. So prepare yourself for an interactive encounter with God, as you seek to know Him more.

I am particularly excited about this study, for I have seen many people find the answers to life's questions as they have gone through the material. I have watched Kathy develop this study over several years, allowing individuals on a search for truth to shape its content. After all, the questions that people are asking are the ones that need to be answered. The fruit of this study is that scores of people have entered a relationship with God and are experiencing abundant life. I know that to be true for I was Kathy's pastor for many years. And I watched her communicate biblical truth to people who had neither previously been to church nor opened a Bible.

So don't be intimidated or feel like you don't know enough about the Bible. This study was written for you. Kathy will guide you very carefully and purposefully through a basic understanding of life's purpose, according to the Bible. I hope you will relate to the personal stories and find yourself pleasantly surprised by many insightful comments along the way. And by the end of the study, you will know enough to make an informed decision about life and your relationship to God.

You are about to have a life-changing experience. So don't rush through the material and shortchange yourself. Take advantage of the opportunity you have been given to address your questions about God and life. You will not be disappointed...you will be set free.

—Dr. Mel Blackaby
senior pastor, First Baptist Church, Jonesboro, Georgia
coauthor, *A God Centered Church*

Acknowledgments

This material was first developed to meet a need at Bow Valley Baptist Church in Cochrane, Alberta. People who weren't familiar with the Bible wanted to study it. We provided a study guide to get them started.

Many people contributed along the way as the material was initially written and taught. My friend and coteacher Gina Blackaby was a constant source of wisdom, encouragement, and prayer. Dr. Jimmy Cobb, my theology professor, double-checked the doctrine. My dear friend Susan Booth not only helped me lead, she also led additional groups and offered valuable insight to improve the study. Wayne, my sweet husband, joined me in teaching several groups and helped keep me from getting too "churchy." Numerous others invited friends, participated in the class, and provided prayer support. Special thanks to Philip and Sabine Koster, Bo and Tonya Stevens, Craig and Judy McPherson, and Pastor Mel Blackaby.

I am grateful to the staff of New Hope Publishers for their faith in me and this material. Their commitment to seeking God's will and direction in every endeavor is a challenge and an encouragement to me.

Introduction

You've picked up this study because you want to know more about God. Be assured, God wants you to know Him. He promises to be found by anyone who earnestly seeks Him. I have experienced the presence of God in my own life. I have witnessed His activity in the lives of many others. Each person's journey is unique. It is a privilege to walk along with you for a while on yours.

This 12-session study called *God's Truth Revealed* is designed to present the basic beliefs of Christianity. Our textbook is the Bible. The Spirit of God will be our teacher.

Although a small group setting is optimal for this study, it can also be done on your own. If you are doing the study in a group, please take time to read the lesson and answer the questions before the group session. Each lesson should take about 30 to 45 minutes to complete. This small time commitment will greatly increase the opportunity for God to teach you about Himself.

You'll find these parts and more in this study:

Personal Stories: Each session includes the true spiritual journey of someone who became a Christian as an adult. These stories demonstrate how God works uniquely and personally in each individual's life. You may or may not find some common ground between their lives and yours, but I am certain you will be encouraged by the hope and purpose God has given each of them. The stories and details are factual, but names have been changed in some cases.

FIND OUT MORE: At the end of each lesson is a bonus section entitled "Find Out More." I encourage you to complete this section a day or two after each group session. Not only will the truths you learned in that session be reinforced, but you will also begin to develop a habit of spending regular time in the Bible.

Churchy Words Dictionary: There are some helpful tools in the back of this book I hope you will use. On page 149 is a "Churchy Words Dictionary." These words, rich in meaning for Christians, are used in churches regularly. Unfortunately, some people who have been in church a long time mistakenly assume most people are familiar with them. Many of these words are defined in the sessions, but you can also look them up anytime in the dictionary.

Guides and Plans: Various Bible reading guides and Scripture memory plans are also included in this book. Regular Bible reading and Scripture memorization encourage spiritual growth. Therefore, many Christians find these types of tools beneficial as they seek to deepen their relationship with God.

There are no prerequisites for this study except a real desire to know the truth about God. Ask Him to reveal Himself to you.

. . . .
. . . .
. . . .
. . . .
. . . .
. . . .

Where Do I Begin?

*A*ny number of events or circumstances may have brought you to this study. You may be exploring Christianity for the first time. Perhaps you are ready to really *know* God, not just know *about* Him. Or maybe you are a new Christian and desire a strong biblical foundation on which to build your faith. This study is for you, whatever your personal situation might be.

I encourage you to explore the claims of Christianity with me for the next 12 weeks. Questions and even skepticism are welcome. All that is necessary is a real desire to know God. Are you willing to let God show you who He is and how He wants to relate to you? The fact that you are involved in this study is proof God is at work in your life. The Bible says no one can come to God unless God draws them. (See John 6:44.)

True Christianity is knowing God in a personal way. Christianity boldly claims there is only one way to know God. Of course, so do other religions. Are they all right? Or has God established one way that is *the* way to know Him? And how can we know which is the one true way?

Let's begin our investigation of Christianity by laying a foundation we will build on over the weeks ahead. The following three concepts are a good place to start:

1. A supreme, divine being we call God does, in fact, exist.
2. God has revealed Himself to humanity through the Bible, which is God's authoritative Word to us for faith and life.
3. Christianity stands out among all other religions because of Jesus and His claims about Himself.

You don't have to believe these statements wholeheartedly or accept them without question in order to participate in this study. What is necessary is a desire to know the truth. Now let's take a closer look at these three statements.

Beginning Point for Faith: Believing in the Existence of God

Everybody puts faith in something. Every person lives his or her life based on some kind of belief system. Because I believe my car will start in the morning I put gasoline in it and plan on using it to get where I need to go tomorrow.

Q: What are some things in which people put their faith?

Q: What does it mean to "have faith" in something or someone?

Q: What are some practical ways people demonstrate this kind of faith?

Where does faith in God come from? It is not a feeling we can produce within ourselves. The Bible says that faith is a gift to an individual from God. (See Ephesians 2:8–9.) Are you receptive to this gift? Are you willing to let God convince you He is real?

Having faith in God does not mean we go through life with our fingers crossed, wondering if what we decided to believe is really true. Hebrews 11:1 says, *"Now faith is being sure of what we hope for and certain of what we do not see."* This Bible verse tells us we can have a firm confidence in God and His promises. We may not *see* many of God's promises right now because they are still yet to happen; or they are spiritual, not physical realities. However, we can live our lives *convinced* He will do what He says.

Additionally, faith is not illogical, blind acceptance. God can stand up under any scrutiny and investigation. One purpose of this study is to provide you with facts and information to support your faith. Living a life of faith does not mean we will never have questions about God and His ways. It does mean that when we do have questions we can trust in the One who has all the answers.

Q: Use the discussion above to write a definition for faith in your own words.

A life of faith is the way of life that pleases God. Hebrews 11:6 says, *"And without faith it is impossible to please God, because anyone who comes to him must believe that he exists and that he rewards those who earnestly seek him."* A relationship with God starts with faith. But that is just the beginning. This verse promises that God will begin to reveal Himself to us when we believe He exists and earnestly seek after Him. We can begin the process of knowing God by acknowledging His existence and seeking to know Him more and more. As we continue in this study, we will explore the relational nature of having faith in the God that exists.

God Makes Himself Known: Trusting in the Authority of the Bible

How important is this book we call the Bible? A wide and diverse range of ideas exists about the nature of the Bible. Christians believe God inspired it to reveal Himself and His ways to mankind. But can we trust what it says? Should it make a difference in our lives?

Q: What are some of the different ways people view the Bible today? Examples: "It's fictional." Or, "It's outdated."

If God does indeed exist and desires a relationship with every individual, He must have also made a way for us to come to know Him. Christians believe individuals can come to know God through His written Word, the Bible. The Bible is also referred to as God's Word and Scripture.

Although the actual manuscripts were written over many centuries by numerous human hands, the Bible has survived the test of time. In fact, there is more evidence for the reliability of the Bible than for any other ancient writing.

The Bible was written over a period of about 1,500 years by more than 40 different human authors in three different languages. No original manuscripts of the Bible exist today. Just like other ancient documents written on perishable materials, the Bible has been preserved over the centuries through oral transmission or copies. So how can we be certain that what God initially gave us is what we have today? There is very strong evidence to support the belief that the Bible has been wonderfully and miraculously preserved.

The Old Testament
Texts: Up until the middle of the twentieth century, the oldest known copy of the Old Testament, referred to as the Masoretic Text, was from about A.D. 900. However, this changed when the Dead Sea Scrolls were discovered in 1947. The oldest of these manuscripts dates back to about 150 B.C., a thousand years older than the Masoretic Text. When the Masoretic Text was compared with the Dead Sea Scrolls it was found to be 95 percent accurate. And the 5 percent discrepancy is due to spelling differences and other minor variations, according to scholars such as Gleason Archer, whose research Dan Story cites in his helpful book *Defending Your Faith.* (See "Recommended Resources," pp. 163–66.)

Archaeology: The Old Testament has been proven historically reliable time and again. For example, archeological digs around Jericho support the biblical story found in Joshua 6.

The New Testament

Texts: More than 24,000 complete and partial copies of the New Testament exist. This is far more than any other ancient document. For example, only 643 copies exist of Homer's *Iliad*. And between these 24,000 copies of the New Testament there is only a 0.5 percent variation. Among the copies of the *Iliad* there is a 5 percent variation (a variation 10 times greater than for the New Testament). Check out Josh McDowell's book, *Evidence That Demands a Verdict,* for more facts and a discussion of these variations.

Time Span: There is a gap from 30 to 60 years between the actual occurrence of the events in the New Testament and when they were written down. In comparison, there is a 500-year gap between Buddha's death and the actual recording of his sayings. Additionally, the New Testament has the shortest time period of any ancient document between existing copies and the date of the originals—just 25 years. In comparison, there is a 500-year span between Homer's original *Iliad* and the oldest existing copy. (See Story, *Defending Your Faith.*)

Not only is the Bible a trustworthy source of information, it is a powerful, spiritual book that can change our day-to-day lives. Find and read 2 Timothy 3:16–17 in your Bible or read it from the margin. (See also "Navigating Your Way Through the Bible," p. 20.)

> *All Scripture is God-breathed and is useful for teaching, rebuking, correcting and training in righteousness, so that the man of God may be thoroughly equipped for every good work.*
> —2 Timothy 3:16–17

In verse 16 of the passage, the Greek word *theopneustos* is used to describe Scripture. It can be translated as "God-breathed" or "divinely inspired." According to Dr. Spiros Zodhiates in *The Complete Word Study New Testament* the word refers to that process by which God directed the writing of the Bible through human beings.

Q: What are some of the uses for Scripture mentioned in this Bible passage?

Hebrews 4:12 provides even more insight into the nature of the Bible. It says, *"For the word of God is living and active. Sharper than any double-edged sword, it penetrates even to dividing soul and spirit, joints and marrow; it judges the thoughts and attitudes of the heart."* God can use the Bible to change an individual and affect his or her life.

Q: Do you feel the Bible might be of benefit to your own life? If so, how?

The passage in Hebrews says that God's Word is not static, time-bound, or general. God's Word is living and active. It is able to penetrate the hearts of individuals and judge their thoughts and motives.

This is just a sampling of the things the Bible says about itself. The Bible claims to be the Word of God revealed to humanity through individuals God inspired to physically write the words. The Bible also claims authority and truth about how God chooses to relate to us and how we should live in response to Him.

How do you feel about these claims? How do these claims the Bible makes about itself compare with the way the world views the Bible? How can you know what is true? Begin to read the Bible. Be open to God showing you truth through His Word working in your own life.

Navigating Your Way Through the Bible

How It's Put Together

- Two main parts—the Old Testament and the New Testament. The Old Testament covers the time period from Creation until about 400 years before Jesus. The New Testament begins with the birth of Jesus. Its focus is His life, death, and resurrection. The New Testament also covers the beginning and spread of Christianity during the first century A.D.

- Individual books—each Testament is further divided into books. Some books are historical, covering a particular time period or event. Others are poetry or prophecy. Still others are letters written to a person or group of people for a specific purpose.

- Chapters and then verses—these divisions were not in the original writings. An editor added them later to make finding a specific passage easier.

Finding a Biblical Reference
Example: Ephesians 2:8–9

Turn to the list of Bible books or table of contents located in the front of your Bible. Find the Book of Ephesians in the list. Note whether it is in the Old or New Testament. The list will provide the page number where the book begins.

Turn to the beginning of the Book of Ephesians. The first number (2:) before the colon is the chapter number. When you open the Bible, the larger numbers mark the chapters. Find the second chapter. The numbers after the colon (8–9) represent the verses. Now looking at the smaller numbers in the text, find and read verses 8 and 9.

God's Ultimate Revelation: Jesus Christ Sets Christianity Apart

The Bible teaches that Jesus Christ is God's ultimate revelation of Himself. In fact, it's Jesus who makes Christianity unique among all the religions of the world. Jesus said the only way a person can know God is through Him. Christians believe this to be true. If this is true, it makes all other efforts to find God futile and empty—merely religion, not a relationship with a living God. Aren't Jesus's claims worth investigating?

There came a point in Jesus's life when He knew He would soon be physically leaving His followers. He wanted to equip them for His departure, so He took an evening to reinforce some of the important truths they would need later.

If you were going away for a time and leaving the ones you love and care for, what would you say to them? Wouldn't you tell them the things that were most important for them to know? Wouldn't you share information they couldn't get along without?

Read John 14:5–10. Find it in your Bible or read it in the margin.

This conversation between Jesus and His disciples took place the night before Jesus was crucified. Jesus had spent the entire evening talking with His closest followers, sharing vital information.

Q: What does Jesus say about His relationship with the Father?

Q: How can we know what the Father is like?

Q: One prominent worldview is that there are many ways to God. This view asserts that although every world religion is a different path, they eventually all lead to the same place.

Q: What does John 14:6 say about this? How do you feel about this?

If Jesus really is the Way, the Truth, and the Life, then He is "the Way" of access to God the Father. This is not a statement created by intolerant Christians but one that comes from the revealed Word of God. According to the Bible, Jesus is the ultimate revelation or "the Truth" of God to mankind. He shows us God as He can be seen by humanity. Jesus is also "the Life" or the source of life for those who come to Him. Do you believe this is so? Ask God to help you know what is true.

Session Summary

We've laid a foundation for this study by looking at three important concepts of Christianity. First, anyone who desires to know God must believe He exists. Second, the Bible is God's true and authoritative Word to us. Third, Jesus Christ is God's ultimate revelation to mankind and is the only way to the Father.

Again, you do not have to believe these things unquestionably to continue in this study. However, please consider the truth of these three statements. When you grasp these truths this study will begin to grow in personal relevance on a daily basis.

• •

Personal Story:
Are You There, God?

God does not exist. There is nothing after death. Life is about what you can get for yourself.

Victor grew up hearing and believing these things.

He was two years old when his mom abandoned him, his two-month-old brother, and his dad. For the next 15 years, Victor's military father raised the boys in "boot camp." These years were hard and often lonely for Victor and his brother.

Victor recalls a few particularly difficult times when he wondered if maybe there really was a God. "I was open to getting any help I could. But if God was calling me, why did He allow suffering? Looking back now, it does seem that God was always whispering to me."

Although Victor consciously shunned organized religion, God, and Jesus in particular, he remembers having an interest in "spiritual" things. As a young adult, he investigated Taoism, Buddhism, and other Eastern religions.

Victor also became involved in the party scene and drug activity. He even dealt drugs for a while in high school. Victor indulged in any activity that might bring pleasure and fulfillment. Instead, he discovered these things brought just the opposite. "They did not satisfy. They did not make me happy," Victor reveals.

At 21 years old, Victor was married with a baby. He and his wife, Chelsey, had both discovered what didn't satisfy in life. Now they wanted to try something different. A house, kids, and family life felt right. They wanted to grow up and be "good people."

Dan and Amber, their new neighbors, seemed to have life figured out. They had everything—a great home, kids, and a dog with puppies. Just one problem. Dan and Amber were *Christians*. Victor soon discovered Dan was just a regular guy—even though he was a Christ follower. The two men began to hang out together. Occasionally Dan would talk about Jesus, but there was no pressure. In fact, Dan's faith was a novelty to Victor, a point of interest to investigate.

When Dan and Amber invited Victor and Chelsey to church they agreed. Chelsey also joined a Bible study for women. Soon after, she committed her life to Jesus. Still skeptical, Victor moved slowly. He now believed God existed, but he did not know what to do with Jesus.

Over the next year, Victor found creative reasons to miss church while Chelsey attended. However, he spent a lot of time lying awake at night wondering what would happen when he died. In addition, there were changes in Chelsey that he could not ignore. Her faith was vital and growing. She had new patience. She approached challenges with strength of character and wisdom. Victor knew it was due to Chelsey's relationship with God.

Finally, Victor agreed to try a Bible study. The emotional reaction he had to Jesus's teachings surprised him. Victor was drawn to them in a way he could not explain.

Victor reflects, "This was different from anything I had 'analyzed' before. Deep down I had a spiritual hunger. I believed Jesus could meet that need. It felt right." Through a physicist in the Bible study group, God opened Victor's eyes to understand that faith is not illogical or unscientific. Victor, now ready to become a Christian, gave his life to Jesus.

After that, a lot of things in Victor's life changed. He now knows God exists because he has a personal relationship with Him. He stopped searching for fulfillment because he found it in Jesus. Victor no longer lives for himself because he lives to please Jesus. And he doesn't wake up at night anymore and wonder what will happen when he dies—Victor knows he'll spend eternity with Jesus. (Read about Chelsey, Victor's wife, in session 8.)

• •

✑ FIND OUT MORE ✑

NOTE: The "Find Out More" section of each session is designed to be used at home between your group times. I encourage you to take time to read the Scriptures and answer the questions each week. Give God the opportunity to speak to you through the Bible. God is personal and relational. He wants you to know Him.

The 119th chapter of the Old Testament Book of Psalms has a lot to say about God's Word. Find and read Psalm 119:9–16 in your Bible.

Q: How does the writer treat God's Word?

Q: What has the writer done with God's Word?

Q: What were the results?

Q: How does the writer feel about God's Word? (vv. 14, 16)

Read Psalm 119:33–37.

Q: What does the writer ask God to do for Him concerning His Word?

Read Psalm 119:89–91.

Q: What qualities of God's Word do you find here?

Q: What role do you feel God's Word could play in your life?

Who Is God?

*M*y friend Dana is a great cook. Everything she makes is not only delicious, it's gorgeous, too. On my 40th birthday she made me a cake—mocha madness. The cake was extremely moist and tasted of chocolate with a hint of coffee. The icing, which was creamy and smooth, was spread all over the cake and between its three layers. The top was decorated with silk flowers, coffee beans, and candles. I was wowed!

To help you understand that Dana is a great cook, I described how her cake tasted and looked. I gave you the end result of her talent. I did not describe a detailed procedure of how she made the cake and what pans and utensils she used. However, describing the appearance and taste of the cake will tell you about the one who made it.

The Bible has a similar purpose with its account of creation in the Book of Genesis, the first book of the Old Testament. *"The heavens declare the glory of God; the skies proclaim the work of his hands"* (Psalm 19:1). The biblical story does not attempt, nor does it intend, to explain how God created. The purpose is for us to recognize God as the source of all things. Scientifically, there is sufficiently greater evidence in support of an Intelligent Designer behind the universe than there is against it. In *The Case for Faith*, author

Lee Strobel, a journalist and former atheist, investigates the issue of evolution versus creation by interviewing leading scientists. He discovered that more and more contemporary scientists are conceding to purposeful creation over chance. (See the inset "Doubting Darwinism" on p. 30.)

This session will explore the truths of God as Creator and His right of authority over all His creation. While other world religions acknowledge similar beliefs, Christianity is set apart by its claims about Jesus. As we will see in this session, the Bible teaches that Jesus was not only involved in the creation of the world; He also has authority over it.

God Is the Creator: Recognizing the Source of All Things

The beginning of time was not the beginning of God. Before time existed God was. God established time as we know it when He made the universe. This idea raises many questions our human minds are unable to answer. There are, however, many things we can understand about God as Creator.

Find Genesis 1:1 to 2:3 in your Bible or read it in the margin on this page.

Q: What did God create on each day of creation?

1st **LIGHT**

2nd **SKY**

3rd **LAND - VEGETATION FLORA -**

4th **STARS -**

5th **- CREATURES OF THE SEA + SKY FAUNA - START**

6th **- CREATURES OF THE LAND INCLUDING HUMANS**

God created the universe and everything in it. The word *created* in Genesis 1:1 is translated from the Hebrew word *bara*. In the Bible, this particular form of the word describes an activity only God can do. According to *The Complete Word Study Old Testament*, edited by Warren Baker, the use of *bara* is restricted to divine activity because *bara* implies creation without the use of any material.

Reading the account of creation, I am struck by its scope. God not only laid down the foundation for the entire universe, He also

In the beginning God created the heavens and the earth.

Now the earth was formless and empty, darkness was over the surface of the deep, and the Spirit of God was hovering over the waters. And God said, "Let there be light," and there was light. God saw that the light was good, and He separated the light from the darkness. God called the light "day," and the darkness he called "night." And there was evening, and there was morning—the first day.

And God said, "Let there be an expanse between the waters to separate water from water." So God made the expanse and separated the water under the expanse from the water above it. And it was so. God called the expanse "sky." And there was evening, and there was morning—the second day.

And God said, "Let the water under the sky be gathered to one place, and let dry ground appear." And it was so. God called the dry ground "land," and the gathered waters he called "seas." And God saw that it was good.

Then God said, "Let the land produce vegetation: seed-bearing plants and trees on the land that bear fruit with seed in it, according to their various kinds." And it was so. The land produced vegetation: plants bearing seed according to their kinds and trees bearing fruit with seed in it according to their kinds. And God saw that it was good. And there was evening, and there was morning—the third day.

And God said, "Let there be lights in the expanse of the sky to separate the day from the night, and let them serve as signs to mark seasons and days and years, and let them be lights in the expanse of the sky to give light on the earth." And it was so. God made two great lights—the greater light to govern the day and the lesser light to govern the night. He also made the stars. God set them in the expanse of the sky to give light on the earth, to govern the day and the night, and to separate light from darkness. And God saw that it was good. And there was evening, and there was morning—the fourth day.

And God said, "Let the water teem with living creatures, and let birds fly above the earth across the expanse of the sky." So God created the great creatures of the sea and every living and moving thing with which the water teems, according to their kinds, and every winged bird according to its kind. And God saw that it was good. God blessed them and said, "Be fruitful and increase in number and fill the water in the seas, and let the birds increase on the earth." And there was evening, and there was morning—the fifth day.

And God said, "Let the land produce living creatures according to their kinds: livestock, creatures that move along the ground, and wild animals, each according to its kind." And it was so. God made the wild animals according to their kinds, the livestock according to their kinds, and all the creatures that move along the ground according to their kinds. And God saw that it was good.

Then God said, "Let us make man in our image, in our likeness, and let them rule over the fish of the sea and the birds of the air, over the livestock, over all the earth, and over all the creatures that move along the ground."

So God created man in his own image, in the image of God he created him; male and female he created them.

God blessed them and said to them, "Be fruitful and increase in number; fill the earth and subdue it. Rule over the fish of the sea and the birds of the air and over every living creature that moves on the ground."

Then God said, "I give you every seed-bearing plant on the face of the whole earth and every tree that has fruit with seed in it. They will be yours for food. And to all the beasts of the earth and all the birds of the air and all the creatures that move on the ground—everything that has the breath of life in it—I give every green plant for food." And it was so.

God saw all that he had made, and it was very good. And there was evening, and there was morning—the sixth day.

Thus the heavens and the earth were completed in all their vast array.

By the seventh day God had finished the work he had been doing; so on the seventh day he rested from all his work. And God blessed the seventh day and made it holy, because on it he rested from all the work of creating that he had done.

—Genesis 1:1–2:3

concentrated on the smallest of details such as the seeds inside an apple.

Q: What must God be like to have created such a vast yet detailed universe? INTUITIVE - GENEROUS - FAITHFUL (ALL IN- I GIVE IT ALL TO YOU) - PERFECTIONIST

Q: What does the order of His creation reveal about God the Creator? - LOGICAL

- SLIGHT DISAGREEMENT ON DAY 5+6

As each day of creation was completed we are told, *"God saw that it was good."* Can you imagine the difference between God's good and our good? I have made many "good" but imperfect creations over the years. The first time I attempted to wallpaper a room is a prime example. Not only did I have to reorder paper twice, several sections had to be pieced together. It cost me three days and my sanity to paper one small bathroom. But I must say it looks pretty good—unless you look closely. In contrast, when God declares something to be good you can be assured it is perfect.

Doubting Darwinism

Contrary to what you may have heard, every reputable scientist does *not* believe evolution holds all the answers to the complexities of life. In fact, more than 400 scientists from around the world have signed their names to an official statement entitled "A Scientific Dissent from Darwinism." The statement reads:

*We are skeptical of claims for the ability of random muta-
tion and natural selection to account for the complexity of
life. Careful examination of the evidence for Darwinian
theory should be encouraged.*

The list was launched by the Discovery Institute in 2001
as a response to a series aired on PBS called *Evolution*. The
show claimed that no scientists disagreed with Darwinian
evolution. Yet, the dissent includes scientists from every
field of study. Even more significant, those who sign the
dissent do so on scientific grounds, not religious ones. And
the list keeps growing as new research continues to reveal
the inadequacy of Darwinian theory to account for the vast
amount of information content in living things. (For more
information, visit www.discovery.org and its link to www.
dissentfromdarwin.org. You can also download a copy
of the list at http://www.discovery.org/scripts/viewDB/
filesDB-download.php?command=download&id=660.)

God Owns His Creation:
Acknowledging His Rights of Ownership

The biblical writers consistently acknowledge God as Creator, the
source of everything that exists. They also acknowledge that God
loves everything He has made. The Bible says in Psalm 145:17,
"The Lord is righteous in all his ways and loving toward all he has made."
It's not surprising that over and over again the human response to
the Creator includes awe and praise.

Q: Can you think of other ways we should respond to God as Creator?
THANKFUL - TRUSTFULL

The Bible says, *"The earth is the Lord's and everything in it, the world,
and all who live in it; for he founded it upon the seas and established it upon
the waters"* (Psalm 24:1–2). As Creator, God makes some significant
claims on His creation.

Q: What claim does God make on creation? Why can God alone make this claim? *- ALL WAS (VERY) GOOD -- INDICATING PERFECTION -*

Q: How do you feel about the idea that God has the right of ownership over your life because He is Creator? *IM OK WITH THAT - THIS HAS ONLY COME ABOUT A FEW YEARS AGO*

Think about something you own. You may picture a house or a car. Although you have the privileges of ownership there are also certain responsibilities involved. Our family, for example, has a yellow Lab named Boone. We chose his name. We decide whether he will be inside the house or outside. (And it's outside when it's my choice.) We decide if he will go with us on trips or stay at a boarding kennel. But we also have to make sure he has plenty of food and water. We have to keep him up on all his shots. And we have to make sure he stays in our yard and out of the neighbor's. This is sometimes easier said than done! The privilege of owner-ship also brings responsibility.

Q: Make two lists below. Note the privileges of ownership on one side and the responsibilities that come with ownership on the other.

Rights / Privileges	Responsibilities
HIKING IN MTS	*- STAY ON TRAIL - REDUCE IMPACT ON FLORA + FAUNA -*
	- PACK OUT GARBAGE
	- REPORT ISSUES -
OWNING A HOUSE	*- PAY MTG - BILLS ETC.*
	- MAINTAIN TO KEEP CURB APPEAL
	- KIND + TO NEIGHBOURS -
	- WORK TOGETHER

Q: If God has the right of ownership over you, how do you think
He will also fulfill His responsibility?
-- HELP IN TROUBLING TIMES
- KEEP ME CHALLENGED - ABLE BODY + MIND
- ALLOW ME SUCCESSFUL ENDEVERS

Truths About Jesus: He Is the Source and Authority for Life

Other world religions agree that some god created the world.
They also agree that their god or gods have authority over what
has been created. However, Christianity is once again unique in its
beliefs about Jesus Christ. In the last session, we read John 14:6
in which Jesus said, *"I am the way, the truth and the life. No one comes
to the Father except through me."* How can Jesus make such a claim?
Jesus also said, *"All authority in heaven and earth has been given to me"*
(Matthew 28:18). If this is true, it helps us understand His claim
that He is the only way to God and not one way among many.

As humans, why are we resistant to advice from ones who
really know what they are talking about? There is only one road
you can take to get to the street where I live. Many times I've tried
to give directions to people, but they are so sure they know how
to get here they say they "don't need them." More times than not I
end up getting a phone call from a visitor who can't find his or her
way to my house.

Does Jesus know what He is talking about when He claims to
be the only way to God?

Read Colossians 1:15–17 in the margin. (These verses refer to
Jesus; see Colossians 1:13.)

Verse 15 says that Jesus is the "firstborn" over all creation. This means Jesus
is preeminent in rank and authority.

Q: Underline the statements about
Jesus found in these verses. Do
you feel this adds any weight to
His claim that He is the only way
to God?

> *He is the image of the invisible God,
> the firstborn over all creation. For
> by him all things were created: things
> in heaven and on earth, visible and
> invisible, whether thrones or powers
> or rulers or authorities; all things
> were created by him and for him.
> He is before all things, and in him all
> things hold together.*
> —Colossians 1:15–17

Q: What place does Jesus have in your life right now? What do you think would be different if you gave Jesus first place in your life?

- GIVEN ME A GOAL - FOCUS - TO GET TO KNOW GOD ~ BE BETTER - #1 ? ~··

Session Summary

As Creator, God is the source of everything that exists. As Creator, God has the right of ownership to everything that exists, including you and me. God the Father created all things through Jesus the Son. The Father has given Jesus authority over all things, including you and me. (See Matthew 28:18 and John 3:35.) How do these facts affect what you now think about Jesus? Consider what impact these truths about Jesus should have on your life.

• •

Personal Story:
It's All about God

Twenty years ago, making money and gratifying his self-centered desires were Hermann's life goals.

Hermann thought he had given God a try. Raised going to church, he truly believed in God. He even recalls, as a young man, having a desire to know Him, but God seemed too distant. Hermann reflects on that time, "I remember praying my last prayer around the age of 19 or 20. The gist was this, 'God, I know you're real. I've tried to know you, but it obviously doesn't work for me. I can't do it. If you want me, you'll have to come to me.'"

Old enough to make his own decisions, Hermann left God behind and began to pursue his goals. But after nearly 15 years of living for himself, Hermann was miserable. Everything he thought would bring satisfaction failed to deliver and his marriage was falling apart. That's when God chose to answer Hermann's prayer.

God spoke to him in the middle of a business presentation. It was as loud and clear as if it had been audible. "Hermann, I love you. I love you more than you'll ever love your own son. Everything you've ever looked for you'll find in Me."

Hermann felt stunned. The people and the voices in the room receded as the reality of what happened hit him. God had come to Hermann. He responded immediately to God's invitation and gave his life completely to Jesus.

Hermann began voraciously reading the Bible. He could not get enough of God's Word. "I just pored into it and it poured into me," he explains.

Immediately Hermann's perspective on who had authority over his life shifted. "I was reoriented to the truth that this is God's world. He is the Author and Sustainer of life. I am accountable to God for every moment."

Before becoming a Christian, Hermann never questioned the existence of God. But he had not yielded his life to God's authority. "I knew in my head that God had the right of ultimate authority over my life. But I did not submit to it."

Because Hermann's upbringing in the church was strict and legalistic, he came to think of God as a cruel dictator. But after giving his life to Jesus, Hermann came to understand who God is. "He is a good God that wants my best. He is perfect love. When I began to submit to the authority of God I experienced that the Lord is good."

Hermann recognizes that acknowledging God's right to authority is a huge stumbling block for many people. "People have such a struggle submitting to the authority of God. They want to say there are many ways to God. But that's not right. Consider a guy who starts his own company. He finances it. He hires the people. He is the source of the company. That guy gets to call the shots. God created the world. He gets to call the shots."

• •

Get to know your Creator! Spend time with God in His Word, the Bible, finding out more about our Creator God.

Find and read Isaiah 40:21–31 in your Bible.

Q: How do these verses describe God in relation to what He has created? (vv. 21–25)

HE IS SOVERN – HE GAVE IT ALL TO YOU AND CAN TAKE IT AWAY

POINT BLANK THIS IS WHAT IT IS – WAKE UP
└ HE CREATED – WE ARE HIS CREATION

↳ AND RULES OVER US.

Q: What kind of authority does God have over His creation? *ALL* Why is this good for us? (vv. 23–26)

→ Gives us a sense of obedience

Q: According to verse 26, God, the Creator, controls the stars by His great power. Do you think a God this big understands you and cares about your well-being? (vv. 27–31)

___✔ Yes   ____No   _____Sometimes

Q: What characteristics can we count on from God, the Creator? (vv. 28–29)

He will always be there –
everlasting love.
– He will help those who believe in him

God is so big and powerful that the universe came into existence at His command. Yet, He is personal and intimate. He knows you inside and out. He knows your needs, your fears, your hopes and your dreams. Based on this passage what place does God want to have in your life?

Close personal relationship to help you grow.

....
....
....
....
....
....

Why Am I Here?

*W*hen I was a teenager I regularly bought the magazine *Seventeen*. In fact, I focused on trying to look like one of the models on the cover. I worked hard to develop a body that met society's image of perfection. I felt if I didn't succeed, then those around me would not accept me. Unfortunately my quest threw me into a struggle with bulimia. Without a doubt I had been patterning my life after the wrong ideal. Although bulimia did not keep a grip on me for very long, it took another decade of searching before I realized why God chose to create me.

Everyone desires meaning and purpose in life. Do you believe you are here for a reason or that your life is just chance? Do you feel you are left to stumble along on your own and if you're lucky you'll fall into something that gives your life direction? Do you believe there could be a point to all this?

The Bible says God created the earth for it to be inhabited (Isaiah 45:18). People were His main purpose in creation. We were the crowning touch. God, our heavenly Father, made us, His children, in His own image. This distinction sets us apart from all the rest of God's creatures. This session will explore the significance of the fact that humanity was made in the image of God.

We will look specifically at how this truth relates to who we are as people and our purpose for life.

> The LORD God formed the man from the dust of the ground and breathed into his nostrils the breath of life, and the man became a living being.
>
> Now the LORD God had planted a garden in the east, in Eden; and there he put the man he had formed. And the LORD God made all kinds of trees grow out of the ground—trees that were pleasing to the eye and good for food. In the middle of the garden were the tree of life and the tree of the knowledge of good and evil....
>
> The LORD God took the man and put him in the Garden of Eden to work it and take care of it. And the LORD God commanded the man, "You are free to eat from any tree in the garden; but you must not eat from the tree of the knowledge of good and evil, for when you eat of it you will surely die."
>
> The LORD God said, "It is not good for the man to be alone. I will make a helper suitable for him."
>
> Now the LORD God had formed out of the ground all the beasts of the field and all the birds of the air. He brought them to the man to see what he would name them; and whatever the man called each living creature, that was its name. So the man gave names to all the livestock, the birds of the air and all the beasts of the field. But for Adam no suitable helper was found. So the LORD God caused the man to fall into a deep sleep; and while he was sleeping, he took one of the man's ribs and closed up the place with flesh. Then the LORD God made a woman from the rib he had taken out of the man, and he brought her to the man.
>
> The man said, "This is now bone of my bones and flesh of my flesh; she shall be called 'woman,' for she was taken out of man."
>
> For this reason a man will leave his father and mother and be united to his wife, and they will become one flesh. The man and his wife were both naked, and they felt no shame.
>
> —Genesis 2:7–9, 15–25

God Created You in His Image: You Are His Representative

Why you are here? Were you created with a specific purpose in mind? Is there meaning beyond this material, physical life? The best place to begin answering these questions is in Genesis, the first book of the Bible. Chapters 1 and 2 give the account of God's creation of the first man and woman. Here we will find basic truths about humanity that give clarity to our lives today.

Find Genesis 1:26–28 and reread it. (You can also refer to session 2, p. 29.) Now read Genesis 2:7–9, 15–25 in your Bible or read it in the margin. Genesis 1 gives us an overview of the creation of humans while Genesis 2 takes a closer look. The two stories are complementary.

Q: How does the way God created humans differ from the way He created animals in Genesis 1:24–25?

Created humans from an existing object, then used one to create the other – similar to mitosis

According to *The Complete Word Study Old Testament*, the word *man* in Genesis 1:26 is the Hebrew word *adham*. It is used generically here to refer to both genders. Genesis 1:27 clarifies that both man and woman were created in the image of God. Being created in God's image is what sets humans apart from the rest of creation. The Hebrew words translated as *image* and *likeness* indicate that the bearer of the image has a strong similarity to the one he or she represents. However, *likeness* does not mean "sameness." Mankind was created to be like God, but we are not identical to God. (For more on this topic, see Wayne Grudem's *Systematic Theology: Introduction to Biblical Doctrine*, p. 440ff.)

The Bible tells us God is "spirit" in John 4:24. God created humans in His image, and thus we are not just temporal, physical beings. We are spiritual beings. Unlike everything else God created, people have eternal souls. This is what makes it possible for humans to relate to God. It is the soul within a person that is drawn to search for God. The longing within our own spirit can only be satisfied in a relationship with God, who is Spirit. In fact, in Matthew 16:26 Jesus asks a question with only one answer: *"What good will it be for a man if he gains the whole world, yet forfeits his soul?"* The answer is inescapable: A person's soul is more valuable than all the riches the world has to offer (Matthew 16:26). We have a special potential. We were created to be in relationship with our Creator. This is possible because of the soul God has given us.

Being created in the image of God manifests itself in a number of unique ways. Humans are moral creatures; we have a rational nature; we are self-aware and God-aware; and we have a God-given authority and responsibility over creation. But perhaps most important, humans were created as relational beings. We are capable of relating to God and each other. In fact, we are the only part of God's creation that has the capacity to relate to its Creator in an intimate way, even as friends. We were created to be in relationship to God and to reflect His image to the rest of creation.

Q: God breathed into Adam the "breath of life" (Genesis 2:7). In what way is this statement significant?

- Giving him a soul? a persons soul
  is what defines him or her.

Created by Him and for Him: You Were Made to Worship

Why do many people who have achieved worldly success still struggle to find fulfillment and contentment? This dilemma is as old as humanity itself. The Old Testament Book of Ecclesiastes reveals a similar struggle faced by Israel's King Solomon. Solomon pursued happiness and fulfillment in life through human means, such as education and material things. And by human standards he *[up in the air]* was wildly successful. In fact, the whole world at that time knew *[the air]* of Solomon's wisdom and wealth. But in Ecclesiastes 1:2 Solomon concludes that all worldly pursuits are meaningless. Why? *[with wisdom comes sorrow?]*

Find Acts 17:24–28 in your Bible or read it in the margin.

> "The God who made the world and everything in it is the Lord of heaven and earth and does not live in temples built by hands. And he is not served by human hands, as if he needed anything, because he himself gives all men life and breath and everything else. From one man he made every nation of men, that they should inhabit the whole earth; and he determined the times set for them and the exact places where they should live. God did this so that men would seek him and perhaps reach out for him and find him, though he is not far from each one of us. 'For in him we live and move and have our being.' As some of your own poets have said, 'We are his offspring.'"
> —Acts 17:24–28

Q: Underline everything you can find in this passage that describes the nature of the relationship between God and humans. What do you see in this passage that might explain why Solomon did not find meaning in worldly pursuits? *[God determines time for people places etc. - People have no control over their things its in Gods hands]*

Q: Is there anything in this Scripture passage you find comforting? If so, what is it? *[God will decide when I die.]*

[God will let me know what my purpose is, smack me on the back of my head]

The Bible clearly tells us why we are here. We were made *by* God and *for God* (Colossians 1:16). He created us for His glory (Isaiah 43:7). God wants us to reach out to Him (Acts 17:27). Our purpose in life is to fulfill the role for which we were created—to glorify and worship the Creator in a relationship with Him.

I have an unusual hobby that my husband feels is pointless. I collect unique salt and pepper shakers. They all have some kind of significance to me. For instance, from my home state of Louisiana, I have a set of jazz players. The salt shaker man is playing a trumpet and the pepper shaker man is a saxophone player. If you count the Christmas ones, I have more than two dozen sets of shakers. And I'm just getting started. It's a bit strange, I know, but they're very cute. Anyway, since they are mostly for display, only a few sets actually contain salt and pepper. Many times my husband has picked up Snow White and turned her head down, only to find she is empty. He wants to know why we have salt shakers everywhere if they don't contain salt!

What about you? Are you fulfilling your life's purpose through a relationship with God? Or have you missed the point?

God's Purpose for You: As Reflected in Jesus Christ

God created man and woman in His image. Yet, as we will see in the next session, disobedience distorted the image of God in humanity. However, there is one person, Jesus Christ, who is the complete and true image of God. The Bible says Jesus is the exact likeness of God (2 Corinthians 4:4 NLT). This is the reason God wants us to be like Jesus.

"God knew his people in advance, and he chose them to become like his Son" (Romans 8:29 NLT). The truth that God knew his people in advance does not discount the need for us to choose to follow Christ in a relationship. What it does mean is that God reached out to us long before we ever thought about Him. He gave you a desire to know Him. His purpose for you from the very beginning of creation was that through a saving relationship with Him you would become more and more like Jesus, who is the perfect image of God.

Q: Do you sense God is reaching out to you? If so, in what ways? YES – he is making my faith in him stronger – closer to him. – Helping me become a better person.

My son Mark is the spitting image of his father. This really came to my attention several summers ago on a family camping trip. There stood this nine-year-old boy up to his armpits in chest waders. Just like his father. He was anxious to get out of camp and down to the stream. Just like his father. He knew those trout were just waiting to jump on his line and out of the water. Just like his father. Later he returned to camp, absentmindedly leaving the fly rod his father made him down at the stream. Not quite like his father.

The older Mark gets and the more time he spends with my husband, Wayne, the more like him Mark becomes. As they relate to each other and share experiences, Mark's attitudes and interests become more and more like Wayne's. Right now Mark isn't the accomplished fisherman his father is, but that's what he wants to be. And every summer he gets a little better.

Session Summary

God created you in His image. This fact gives you worth and makes you unique among God's creation. You, as a human being, are capable of relating to God in a way no other creatures can. Being created in God's image also defines the meaning and purpose of your life. You were made to be God's representative on earth, to reflect His nature in all of your relationships, and bring Him glory as you obediently follow Him. God's ultimate purpose for your life is for you to be just like Jesus, enjoying a relationship in the family of God.

• •

Personal Story:
Created to Worship

Sandi felt a need to worship God long before she became a Christian. Though she rejected the idea of church, even as a child she prayed to the God she instinctively knew existed. "I always felt gratitude and wanted to express it to God. I also knew He was powerful and had my best interests at heart."

Over the years, Sandi's desire to connect with God in prayer increased. Before she understood what it meant to have a relationship with Jesus, Sandi sensed that God deserved her awe and worship. Seeking God in prayer was the way Sandi sought to worship Him.

Although Sandi prayed for decades, she did not truly connect with God until she gave her life to Jesus. It was when Sandi began to attend church with her teenage daughter that she quickly discovered a personal relationship with Jesus Christ was what she'd been missing.

As Sandi puts it, "The flood gates were opened." She immediately joined a Bible study group to learn all she could about her new faith. Then soon after, she was baptized to let other people know about her commitment to Jesus.

Although the Bible tells us God made people to worship Him, many people miss His real purpose for their lives. But Sandi has always known that God is worthy of her respect and praise. "I am meant to worship. If I don't worship, pray, sing, talk to God, then things are not in order. Worship is the heart of my relationship with God," Sandi shares. "When I worship the world fades away and it's just me and God. The joy is indescribable."

Now that Sandi is a Christian, she has no doubt that she connects with God during prayer. "I have a direct link to the most awesome God. He knows everything, but He is willing to sit down and chat with me at any given moment. I am in awe every second I speak to Him." (Read about Ron, Sandi's husband, in session 5.)

* *

God wants you to be like Jesus. But do you know what Jesus is like? Begin to get to know Him by reading about His life and reflecting on what you read.

Read Mark 1:35–39.

Q: What is Jesus doing in verse 35? Why do you think Jesus prayed? *Getting closer to God. Get insite on what He should be doing & where*

Q: Why did Jesus say He came?

Preach the Gospel

Read Mark 1:40–45.

Q: What qualities of Jesus do you find demonstrated by the healing of the man with leprosy?

Compassion —

Read Mark 2:1–12.

Q: What needs did Jesus see in the paralyzed man?

FAITH

Q: What authority did Jesus demonstrate? What does this say about who He is? *forgive his sins. ?*

Q: What was the basis for the man's spiritual healing? (See v. 5.)

What Went Wrong?

I watched him as I waited in the checkout line of the local dollar store. He was about 14 or 15 years old. He knelt in front of a shelf stocked with Harry Potter items. Even as he pretended to examine the deck of playing cards, he glanced around nervously and caught my eye. I immediately knew what he was planning to do. I could see it on his face. He put the cards down and picked up something else. He continued to look around and kept looking back at me. I pretended not to be watching when he picked up the cards again. He quickly slipped the cards into his coat and headed for the door about six feet away.

"Hey!" I shouted in his direction. His hand on the door, he paused and looked at me. "You didn't pay for those!" I said, loud enough for the employees behind the counter to hear. The male clerk quickly took the teen by the arm and confiscated the stolen goods. But then, to my surprise, he allowed him to run out the door to his waiting friends.

The youth knew the cards did not belong to him. And it was obvious by his behavior that he knew it was against the law to take them. So why did he do it? Was it a dare? Whatever the reason, he chose to put himself above the law and do it his way. Frankly, I think he would have been better off if the employees had called the authorities because he would have been confronted with an essential life lesson: actions have consequences. Sometimes facing the consequences of our actions is the best thing for us.

The Bible tells us that God's law is written on everyone's heart (Romans 2:15). When we do something wrong our conscience accuses us, pointing us back to the God who created us. I watched this happen in the face of that young shoplifter. It also happens in my own heart every time I choose my own way over God's. Unfortunately, the more and more we act against God's law, the more our conscience is dulled until it no longer accuses our wrong actions.

Last session we learned man and woman were created in the image of God. Being made in God's image gave Adam and Eve the ability to experience the intimate, fulfilling relationship with their Creator He intended. Perfect harmony existed between God and humans, and between humans and the rest of creation. But something happened that damaged God's perfect creation. This session we will read how Adam and Eve broke God's law for the first time. We will discover the consequences of their disobedience. We will also see what implications our disobedience of God has for our lives.

Humans Disobey God: They Choose Their Own Way

When I was growing up, my younger brother and I just couldn't seem to get along. I did not choose him to be a part of our family. In fact, if I'd had a choice I'd have traded him in for a big sister. Like many siblings, we never played well together. I can even remember a number of physical fights Mom had to break up. Whenever she caught us fighting, her solution was to force us to hug each other and apologize. How I hated those moments! The last thing I felt for him at the time was affection. In fact, even as we hugged I was mentally slugging him. Of course like most sibling rivals, now that we are all grown up we are great friends. And given the choice, I would now choose him to be a member of my family.

God wants us to choose Him. Just like us, Adam and Eve could choose God's way or their own way. Why didn't God create us so we could not disobey Him? God created us with the capacity to have a freely chosen relationship with Him.

Q: What is the nature of freedom? Can true freedom exist without boundaries?

Q: What are some limits or boundaries we have in life?

FINANCES, → TRAVEL → OWNERSHIP
MORALS → THINGS WE DO → BAD

Find Genesis 2:15–17 in your Bible or read it in the margin.

God gave Adam tremendous freedom. Adam was free to choose to eat from almost every tree in the garden. God restricted only one tree from Adam's diet.

Q: Why do you think God imposed this or any restriction on Adam and Eve? And why do you think God did not give restrictions to the animals? *– LESSON OF OBEDIENCE*

> The LORD God took the man and put him in the Garden of Eden to work it and take care of it. And the LORD God commanded the man, "You are free to eat from any tree in the garden; but you must not eat from the tree of the knowledge of good and evil, for when you eat of it you will surely die."
> —Genesis 2:15–17

Q: Do you think the existence of the prohibition could strengthen Adam's relationship to God? If so, how? *YES – SHOWING THAT HE COULD FOLLOW "THE "RULES" SET OUT BY GOD.*

Read Genesis 3:1–8 in your Bible or in the margin.

Most Bible scholars identify the serpent in Genesis 3 with our great adversary Satan or the devil. (See "Satan," p. 49, for more information on our adversary.) Like his encounter with Eve, whenever Satan brings temptation our way it often looks enticing. In fact, the Bible says Satan masquerades as an angel of light (2 Corinthians 11:14). He is crafty and cunning and very experienced at what he does.

> *Now the serpent was more crafty than any of the wild animals the LORD God had made. He said to the woman, "Did God really say, 'You must not eat from any tree in the garden'?"*
>
> *The woman said to the serpent, "We may eat fruit from the trees in the garden, but God did say, 'You must not eat fruit from the tree that is in the middle of the garden, and you must not touch it, or you will die.'"*
>
> *"You will not surely die," the serpent said to the woman. "For God knows that when you eat of it your eyes will be opened, and you will be like God, knowing good and evil."*
>
> *When the woman saw that the fruit of the tree was good for food and pleasing to the eye, and also desirable for gaining wisdom, she took some and ate it. She also gave some to her husband, who was with her, and he ate it. Then the eyes of both of them were opened, and they realized they were naked; so they sewed fig leaves together and made coverings for themselves.*
>
> *Then the man and his wife heard the sound of the LORD God as he was walking in the garden in the cool of the day, and they hid from the LORD God among the trees of the garden.*
>
> —Genesis 3:1–8

Disobedience to God often appears beautiful and satisfying. It can even seem like the "sensible" thing to do. However, disobeying God carries eternal consequences.

Q: What was Satan's method of operation with Eve?

Tempting with gaining Knowledge

Q: What questions and doubts about God and His character did the serpent encourage in Eve's mind?

If God is good will he kill you - Against his character of being good

Q: Why do you think Eve chose to disobey God?

Q: Circle the phrases in the last two paragraphs of the Genesis 3:7–8 sidebar that reveal Adam and Eve immediately experienced guilt and shame as a result of their disobedience.

Eve was not alone in her disobedience. Adam, who was present the entire time, also chose to disobey. They were both responsible for their own actions. They knew what God said yet they both chose their own way over His. They thought they knew better than God.

Unfortunately, my children often decide their way is better than their mother's. Thankfully it is usually something minor. For instance, when Sarah began to do her own laundry, I first gave her instructions about sorting and running the machine. Sarah, though, always looking for shortcuts, threw all her dirty clothes in together. Well, you can guess what happened. All her whites are now pink.

You'd think Sarah would listen to her experienced mother. No, she thought her way was better. Seems ridiculous, but we do the same thing with God all the time. And often the results are more disastrous than a lot of pink underwear.

Satan

Is the serpent in Genesis Satan? Several passages in the Bible point to the serpent of Genesis chapter 3 as closely related to Satan or the devil. Revelation 12:9 and 20:2 call Satan that "old serpent." *The Complete Word Study New Testament* explains that the original word for *Satan* means "adversary" or "opposer." The Bible describes him as the great accuser (Revelation 12:10); the father of lies (John 8:44); the evil one (Matthew 13:19); the god of this age (2 Corinthians 4:4); and more.

Where did Satan come from? Scripture indicates that Satan was originally one of God's angels in heaven. Wanting to be like God, Satan rebelled and swayed a third of God's angels to his side. God expelled them from heaven and Satan and his demons have been attempting to thwart God's purposes since. (See Revelation 12:9–11 and Isaiah 14:12–15.)

What will become of Satan? Many scholars believe Genesis 3:15 is the first of many biblical references to Jesus Christ's ultimate victory over Satan and his power. The Book of Revelation clearly teaches Satan's eternal defeat. (See also Romans 16:20 and Revelation 20:10.)

But the LORD God called to the man, "Where are you?"

He answered, "I heard you in the garden, and I was afraid because I was naked; so I hid."

And he said, "Who told you that you were naked? Have you eaten from the tree that I commanded you not to eat from?"

The man said, "The woman you put here with me—she gave me some fruit from the tree, and I ate it."

Then the LORD God said to the woman, "What is this you have done?"

The woman said, "The serpent deceived me, and I ate."

So the LORD God said to the serpent, "Because you have done this, "Cursed are you above all the livestock and all the wild animals! You will crawl on your belly and you will eat dust all the days of your life. And I will put enmity between you and the woman, and between your offspring and hers; he will crush your head, and you will strike his heel."

To the woman he said, "I will greatly increase your pains in childbearing; with pain you will give birth to children. Your desire will be for your husband, and he will rule over you." To Adam he said, "Because you listened to your wife and ate from the tree about which I commanded you, 'You must not eat of it,' "Cursed is the ground because of you; through painful toil you will eat of it all the days of your life. It will produce thorns and thistles for you, and you will eat the plants of the field. By the sweat of your brow you will eat your food until you return to the ground, since from it you were taken; for dust you are and to dust you will return."

Adam named his wife Eve, because she would become the mother of all the living. The LORD God made garments of skin for Adam and his wife and clothed them. And the LORD God said, "The man has now become like one of us, knowing good and evil. He must not be allowed to reach out his hand and take also from the tree of life and eat, and live forever." So the LORD God banished him from the Garden of Eden to work the ground from which he had been taken. After he drove the man out, he placed on the east side of the Garden of Eden cherubim and a flaming sword flashing back and forth to guard the way to the tree of life.
—Genesis 3:9–24

Find Genesis 3:9–24 in your Bible or read it in the margin.

Q: How did God respond? How did Adam and Eve answer God?

QUESTIONED

- POINTED TO EVE

God describes the consequences of Adam's and Eve's disobedience beginning in verse 14. While the serpent and the ground are both cursed, Adam's and Eve's consequences are not labeled the same way. Rather God is describing the natural results that flow from their disobedience. Notice how Adam's and Eve's disobedience brought consequences to each of their primary areas of responsibility in life.

Q: What were the results of their disobedience?

Q: For Adam?

TOIL

Q: For Eve?

PAIN

This event in the third chapter of Genesis is often referred to as "the fall of man" because it is the record of humanity's first act of disobedience against God. Disobedience toward God is also called *sin*. Various Hebrew and Greek words in the Bible have been translated as the word *sin*. In the Old Testament, the Hebrew word *chata* is frequently used to describe disobedience towards God. It means to "miss the way" or "fail." According to *The Complete Word Study Old Testament, chata* carries the idea of being off-target or coming up short of the goal. *The Complete Word Study New Testament* identifies *hamartia* as the Greek word used for sin. This word for sin, defined as "missing the true goal and scope of life," specifically points to "offense in relation to God."

The "target" or "goal" we miss is the perfect pattern God established for man to follow. God's pattern for us is Jesus (Romans 8:29). Any time our thoughts, attitudes, or behavior do not match the pattern of Jesus, we sin. Often our sin is a result of pride. We choose against God's way and choose our way. This implies we think we know better than God. In other words, we attempt to take God's place.

The sin of Adam and Eve brought consequences that affected all of creation. It damaged every relationship. It broke intimacy and brought shame and blame between Adam and Eve. Harmony no longer existed between humanity and the animal world. Even the ground suffered the consequences of their sin. However, the most significant damage was done to the relationship between God and humanity. Sin erected a wall between the Creator and His human creation.

Man and woman were created uniquely from all the rest of creation. They were created in the image of God. God's intended purpose for them was to bring honor to Him by reflecting His image on earth. This was to be accomplished through an obedient and intimate relationship between humanity and their Creator. Now the relationship was broken.

Sin Is a Universal Problem: It Breaks Our Relationship with God

That first sin of Adam and Eve brought death. We see signs of death in every aspect of God's creation. The Bible says creation was subject to frustration and bound to decay (Romans 8:20–21). But sin also brings spiritual death to humanity. Look back at

Genesis 2:17. God told Adam that if he ate from the tree of the knowledge of good and evil he would die. John 17:3 says eternal life is to know God. Sin breaks our own relationship with God, separating us from Him and eternal life. Sin, therefore, brings spiritual death to us like it did to Adam and Eve.

The Bible describes this condition as being *"dead in transgressions"* or sin (Ephesians 2:5). This is what it means to be *"lost."* Many Christians use this term to define the nature of a person's relationship with God. When we sin, our relationship with God is broken. We are cut off from our Creator, who is the source of life. We are therefore lost or doomed to death because of sin. Only through Jesus Christ can eternal life be found.

Q: Romans 3:23 says: *"For all have sinned and fall short of the glory of God."* Who has sinned according to this verse? Does this include you? Do you agree?

- everyone - yes - yes

Q: This verse describes sin as falling short of the glory of God. *God's glory* refers to the likeness of God that He has intended for each person to reflect in his or her life. Our sin has marred God's image in us.

Q: Based on what you know about humanity being created in the image of God, how can this description broaden our understanding of the meaning of *sin?* - understand is its not only "ACTS" that are sin - but also whats inside the heart - feelings -

The Bible says our sin has separated us from God (Isaiah 59:2). Our sin prevents us from having the relationship with Him for which we were created. Another passage elaborates: *"For the wages of sin is death, but the gift of God is eternal life in Christ Jesus our Lord"* (Romans 6:23).

Every one of us is a sinner and deserves death—eternal separation from God our Creator. The Bible calls this place of eternal death *hell*. The Bible presents hell as a real place of torment that is reserved for Satan, his angels, and anyone who has died outside of a saving relationship with God through Jesus Christ (Revelation 20:10–15). However, God in His infinite grace offers eternal life to us as a gift through Jesus. Over the next few sessions we will look at how the Bible says we can receive this gift.

One Perfect Exception: Yet Jesus Understands Our Struggle

There is only one exception to *"all have sinned."* Jesus faced temptation to sin just like we do. Yet the Bible says He never sinned. (See Hebrews 4:15.) Jesus experienced temptation, but never yielded to it. Therefore He is able to fulfill a unique role no one else can. The writer of the New Testament Book of Hebrews establishes a foundation for Jesus Christ's superiority over all other ways man attempts to establish a relationship with God.

Find Hebrews 4:14–15 in your Bible or read it in the margin.

Here Jesus is described as our High Priest. For the Jews the high priest was the intercessor between the people and God. Remember Jesus's claim. *"I am the way, the truth, and the life. No one comes to the Father except through me"* (John 14:6). Jesus is the way to God and the only intercessor we need.

> Therefore, since we have a great high priest who has gone through the heavens, Jesus the Son of God, let us hold firmly to the faith we profess. For we do not have a high priest who is unable to sympathize with our weaknesses, but we have one who has been tempted in every way, just as we are—yet was without sin.
> —Hebrews 4:14–15

Q: Is it significant to you that Jesus was tempted in every way we are? If so, why?

No – FAITH – having faith in something someone – means they have nothing to prove.

Q: What does it mean to you that Jesus is your mediator (or go-between) with God?

- Finally understanding that.
- We talk to God but not Jesus?
- Understanding that he was the final sacrifice for our sin. Eternally grateful -

Session Summary

Sin is rejecting the authority of God by choosing our own way over His way. This bent toward rebellion, which began in the Garden of Eden, affects all of creation and every relationship. Just like the teen in the dollar store who chose his own way, everyone is a sinner, including you and me. Sin has broken our relationship with God, the source of life, and has brought spiritual death. Jesus completely understands our struggle with sin. In fact, in the upcoming sessions we will see how God has provided a way through Jesus to restore our broken relationship with Him and to receive His gift of eternal life.

* *

Personal Story:
Even Good Guys Need Jesus

Darin was a good guy. All his friends and neighbors would tell you that.

He wasn't opposed to God or church. Darin just didn't feel the need. He lived a good life. He had a nice family. He certainly didn't want anyone trying to convert him.

Herb, one of Darin's neighbors, was a Christian. Herb didn't try to hide his faith but he wasn't pushy either. Darin and Herb became close friends. Darin's wife, Glennie, became close friends with Herb's wife, Kathy. The four of them spent a lot of time together.

The friends began to talk more about spiritual things. Soon, Glennie accepted Kathy's invitation to attend a Bible study at their church. In a matter of weeks, she gave her life to Jesus. The immediate change Darin witnessed in Glennie's character overwhelmed him. Glennie was great before, but after she became a Christian she was more loving, giving, and selfless. Something miraculous had definitely happened to Darin's wife.

Something else happened that increased Darin's interest in Christianity. His father had open-heart surgery. Glennie's new church cared enough to pray for him during the service. Darin felt it was finally time to attend this church and see for himself what was going on there.

Darin really didn't expect much. After all, what could a regular good guy get out of church? But he couldn't have been more wrong. It seemed like the pastor was speaking right to Darin. He wanted to know more so he joined a Bible study class. What he learned from the Bible affected him immediately. "Bible study class felt like therapy. I could feel the presence of God's Spirit. I hungered for God's Word. I just couldn't get enough. The truths in the Bible penetrated deeply and pierced my heart."

During the eight-week Bible study class, Darin realized he needed Jesus. It didn't matter how "good" a guy he was. He wasn't and could never be perfect. He was a sinner. But Jesus offered Darin forgiveness. "I kept asking God, 'Why me, Lord? Why would you save a wretched guy like me after all I've done?' God's answer was, 'Because I love you, Darin.'"

Darin knew he was different. He was forgiven; he belonged to Jesus. Darin doesn't want to be thought of as "a good guy" anymore. He only wants other people to think of him as someone who follows Jesus and wants to please Him. (Read about Glennie, Darin's wife, in session 10.)

• •

The Apostle John wrote three letters, or *epistles*, to early Christians. The first letter is designated as the New Testament Book (or Epistle) of 1 John. John was also one of Jesus's 12 disciples. Jesus chose a group of 12 men to follow Him and assist Him during His earthly ministry. John was an eyewitness to all Jesus said and did while He was on earth. His purpose in writing was so others could experience the fellowship, life, and joy that come from a relationship with Jesus. As you read the following passage notice the themes of "light" and "darkness." Often in the Bible the words *light* and *darkness* are used to refer to the absence of sin and the presence of sin, respectively.

Q: Read 1 John 1:3–10. How is God described? What does this mean considering the statement about light and darkness in the text above? *He is light, - He is not sinfull*

Q: What is our own condition concerning sin?
- Accept it you are sinning & will sin,

Q: What effect has sin had on your relationships? With God? With family? With friends? *- People did not like me as much - separating from the "Good" people*

Q: How can our sin be dealt with? In verse 7, what does Jesus do for us? *- Believe in Jesus - who he was & what he did.*

Q: Do you agree with God that you are a sinner? If you answered yes, write a prayer of confession to Him now.
YES - I know I am a sinner - I believe in Jesus and strive to be more like him.

In the following sessions we will look more closely at how Jesus's death on the Cross paid the penalty for our sins. This makes it possible for us to receive God's forgiveness and gift of eternal life.

How Did God Respond?

*M*y life did not flash before my eyes. I was too concerned about how—or if—I was going to make it back to the beach. Our family trip that day was not supposed to end with me drowning in a riptide.

It was our first day on the beach with our rented boogie boards, and I was the first one in the water. Wanting to catch the waves where they were breaking, I headed away from the shore. By the time I realized they were breaking too far out, the water was over my head. On the board from the waist up, I started kicking to get back to the beach. After a couple of minutes I had not made any progress. In fact, I was farther away from the beach and farther down the shoreline. The board was strapped to my wrist so I let it trail behind me and began to swim. I swam until I was exhausted and swallowing water, but I was even farther from shore. No matter what I did or how hard I worked, I could not save myself.

Seeing I was in trouble, my husband grabbed another board, left the safety of the beach and came to my rescue. My three children watched from shore. I could hear the youngest crying for me. When Wayne reached me, he calmed me down and talked me through riding out the riptide so we could get back to the beach. Moments later I was reunited with my family.

In our last session we learned that *sin* is disobeying God, or choosing our own way over God's way. Sin first entered the world when Adam and Eve disobeyed God, breaking their intimate relationship with Him. Everyone has sinned. (See Romans 3:23.) This sin breaks our relationship with God bringing with it the consequence of spiritual death. (See Romans 6:23.) This means we are lost, separated from God and unable to mend the relationship ourselves. There is a gulf between God and us that we cannot cross. Just like me in the riptide, we can do nothing to save ourselves.

This session we will look at how God responded to our predicament. Since we could not save ourselves, God came to our rescue. We celebrate the anniversary of this great rescue mission every 25th of December.

God Came to Earth: Jesus Is Born

What do you think about when someone mentions Christmas? Do you think about special times with family and friends? Do you think about angels, stars, and a baby named Jesus? The real meaning of Christmas is much more. God Himself embarked on a rescue mission to save sinners—and that includes you and me.

The first four books of the New Testament—Matthew, Mark, Luke, and John—are in English called the Gospels, the word *gospel* being derived from an Old English word meaning "good news." The Gospels record the good news about Jesus and His life. Scholars generally date their written forms between A.D. 50 and A.D. 100. (General consensus places Jesus's birth between 4–6 B.C. and His crucifixion and resurrection between A.D. 29–30.) Two of these writers, Matthew and Luke, recorded events surrounding the birth, which took place approximately 2,000 years ago. Since each wrote about different parts of the story, we'll look at both to get the big picture.

Read Matthew 1:18–25 in the margin.

Matthew tells us that Mary and Joseph were pledged to be married. In their culture, engagement was legally binding. They were considered husband and wife, because their relationship could only be dissolved by divorce or death. Unfaithfulness was considered adultery. In Jewish law the punishment for adultery was death.

In the first chapter of Luke we are told that because Mary found favor with God He chose her to be the earthly mother of His Son Jesus. When an angel came to give her the news, she asked how this was possible since she was a virgin. The angel assured Mary she would become pregnant by the power of God through His Spirit. This would not be an ordinary birth or an ordinary baby.

Imagine Joseph's hurt, fear, and confusion when he learned that Mary was going to have a baby. But God did not leave him in this state. God sent an angel to Joseph to explain the situation and give him some inside information.

> This is how the birth of Jesus Christ came about: His mother Mary was pledged to be married to Joseph, but before they came together, she was found to be with child through the Holy Spirit. Because Joseph her husband was a righteous man and did not want to expose her to public disgrace, he had in mind to divorce her quietly.
>
> But after he had considered this, an angel of the Lord appeared to him in a dream and said, "Joseph son of David, do not be afraid to take Mary home as your wife, because what is conceived in her is from the Holy Spirit. She will give birth to a son, and you are to give him the name Jesus, because he will save his people from their sins."
>
> All this took place to fulfill what the Lord had said through the prophet: "The virgin will be with child and will give birth to a son, and they will call him Immanuel"—which means, "God with us."
>
> When Joseph woke up, he did what the angel of the Lord had commanded him and took Mary home as his wife. But he had no union with her until she gave birth to a son. And he gave him the name Jesus..
>
> —Matthew 1:18–25

Q: Underline all the facts you can find in Matthew 1:18–25 about the baby that will be born.

Names were extremely significant in ancient times. Often they described the person's nature, character, and purpose. *Jesus* means "the Lord helps" or "the Lord saves." These names are vitally important when we think about the concept of being spiritually "lost." Spiritual salvation is delivery from sin and its eternal consequences.

Q: What do you learn about Jesus's nature, character, and purpose from His two names in this passage? Note: The angel announces both of these names to Joseph and gives the meanings.

- He will save people - GOD WILL WALK AMONG US.

In those days Caesar Augustus issued a decree that a census should be taken of the entire Roman world. (This was the first census that took place while Quirinius was governor of Syria.) And everyone went to his own town to register.

So Joseph also went up from the town of Nazareth in Galilee to Judea, to Bethlehem the town of David, because he belonged to the house and line of David. He went there to register with Mary, who was pledged to be married to him and was expecting a child. While they were there, the time came for the baby to be born, and she gave birth to her firstborn, a son. She wrapped him in cloths and placed him in a manger, because there was no room for them in the inn.

And there were shepherds living out in the fields nearby, keeping watch over their flocks at night. An angel of the Lord appeared to them, and the glory of the Lord shone around them, and they were terrified. But the angel said to them, "Do not be afraid. I bring you good news of great joy that will be for all the people. Today in the town of David a Savior has been born to you; he is Christ the Lord. This will be a sign to you: You will find a baby wrapped in cloths and lying in a manger."

Suddenly a great company of the heavenly host appeared with the angel, praising God and saying, "Glory to God in the highest, and on earth peace to men on whom his favor rests."

When the angels had left them and gone into heaven, the shepherds said to one another, "Let's go to Bethlehem and see this thing that has happened, which the Lord has told us about."

So they hurried off and found Mary and Joseph, and the baby, who was lying in the manger. When they had seen him, they spread the word concerning what had been told them about this child, and all who heard it were amazed at what the shepherds said to them. But Mary treasured up all these things and pondered them in her heart. The shepherds returned, glorifying and praising God for all the things they had heard and seen, which were just as they had been told.

—Luke 2:1–20

Joseph obeyed in faith and brought Mary to his home. Together they waited for the arrival of God's promised child. They probably began to prepare things at home in anticipation. However, any plans they'd made were interrupted by the Roman government. At this time in history Rome ruled much of the known world. Caesar required all the Jews to return to their ancestral home to register, probably for tax purposes. Joseph was a descendant of Israel's great king, David, who was from Bethlehem. So late in Mary's pregnancy, the couple traveled to Bethlehem.

Find Luke 2:1–20 in your Bible or read it in the margin.

Q: What would you expect the birth of God's Son to be like? OPULENT

Q: Describe the circumstances of Jesus's birth.

- VERY HUMBLE

There are lots of different ways to announce the birth of a child. I have seen everything from the common card and cigar to chocolate bars with specially designed wrappers. But the first announcement of Jesus's birth was truly unique. God sent angels to a group of shepherds working in the fields. In that day, shepherds were pretty much at the bottom of the Jewish social ladder.

Q: Do you think it is significant that Jesus's birth was first announced to shepherds? Why?

— To let everyone know that they are worthy of - believing in the Lord & not saved for the HIGH PRIEST

Q: What response did this announcement elicit? From the angels? From the shepherds?   *↳ AT FIRST FEAR THEN*

— YAHOO! - PRAISE THE LORD - HE IS HERE

- EXCITEMENT - Go TELL IT ON THE MT.

Q: Three more names for Jesus can be found in the third paragraph of the sidebar (Luke 2:11). Find each one and circle it.

The angel's announcement includes more names for Jesus. *Savior* means "deliverer." *Christ* (Greek) or *Messiah* (Hebrew) means "anointed one." *Lord* means "one who is supreme." For centuries the Jewish people had been waiting for the Messiah. In the Old Testament, through His messengers the prophets, God had promised a deliverer who would come and save His people. Many ages of oppression had caused Israel to look for the anointed one to come in military power and strength. A humble babe was not what the people expected.

Q: What about you? What do you expect from Jesus? How have you responded to His birth?

- TO BE THERE FOR ME

Historical Record of Jesus

The presence of Jesus on earth is historical fact. Jesus is mentioned outside the Bible by secular historians. Following are some examples.

Josephus was a highly significant and respected Jewish historian born in A.D. 37. In his book, *The Antiquities of the Jews*, a history of the Jewish people completed in A.D. 93, Josephus mentions Jesus twice:

1. He relates the Jewish trial and conviction of James, a Christian leader in Jerusalem. James is described as the "brother of Jesus, who was called Christ."

2. There is a lengthier passage about Jesus Himself. It refers to Jesus performing miracles and describes His teaching as winning over many Jews and Greeks. Josephus also reports that Jesus was condemned to die on a cross. The text continues by stating that Jesus appeared "alive again the third day, as the divine prophets had foretold," though some scholars consider this a later Christian addition. The majority of scholars agree that, despite some possible later revisions, at least part of this passage from Josephus is authentic—more than enough to confirm Jesus's existence, even apart from the records of the Gospels. (If you are interested in reading Josephus's entire account, see William Whiston's *The Works of Josephus*. You may also want to refer to the brief and helpful article, http://www.facingthechallenge.org/josephus.php.)

Cornelius Tacitus was a Roman historian. Writing in A.D. 112, he made reference to Jesus's death decreed by the Roman governor Pilate. Further, he describes the subsequent persistence of Jesus's followers in Judea and Rome. You can refer to Tacitus's writings in Josh McDowell's *Evidence that Demands a Verdict.*

God Became Man: Jesus Chose Humble Service

The Books of Matthew and Luke tell us the story of the birth of Jesus from an earthly perspective. However, there is a passage in the New Testament Book of Philippians that gives the story from a heavenly perspective. More than likely this passage of Scripture was a hymn (song of worship) of the early church. Like those early Christians, focusing on what Jesus has done on our behalf can help us internalize God's desire for all His children to be like His Son Jesus. Jesus's life is the supreme example of self-sacrifice, self-denial, and obedience to the Father.

Find Philippians 2:5–11 in your Bible or read it in the margin below.

Verse 6 tells us that Jesus is God, but at a certain point in history, He chose not to cling to this fact, but to take on human form and come to earth in a physical body. This is known as the *incarnation*. This term refers to God becoming "flesh," a human. The incarnation was the long-awaited physical presence of God among His people for the purpose of salvation. The incarnation made Jesus fully human, but it did not change the fact that He was also fully God. This is another great mystery of God that is difficult to understand, but the Bible says it is true. (See Colossians 1:19 and 2:9.) Scripture

Your attitude should be the same as that of Christ Jesus: Who, being in very nature God, did not consider equality with God something to be grasped, but made himself nothing, taking the very nature of a servant, being made in human likeness. And being found in appearance as a man, he humbled himself and became obedient to death—even death on a cross! Therefore God exalted him to the highest place and gave him the name that is above every name, that at the name of Jesus every knee should bow, in heaven and on earth and under the earth, and every tongue confess that Jesus Christ is Lord, to the glory of God the Father. —Philippians 2:5–11 is clear that Jesus is also eternal, existing in heaven before His physical birth (John 1:1–2).

Think about the most opulent place you can imagine. You may picture lots of gold, marble, and silk furnishings. You may hear music playing softly while luscious smells waft from an unseen kitchen. Here you are the master. Now imagine the most humble of circumstances. Perhaps you see a dirt floor and only rice for dinner. Here you are a servant.

Q: Jesus left the glory of heaven. What kinds of things do you think He left behind? — *HIS FATHER —*
being around those who are good
natured & Christians
— ALL LOOKED UP TO HIM.

Q: Think about the fact that God Himself took on human form. What are some of the implications? Include ones from this passage and others you can think of.

Q: What was the result of Jesus's obedience to the Father?
Exalted Him to the highest
place, name & story will
go on forever

Jesus was completely God and completely human. He chose not to take advantage of His divinity, but to humble Himself in complete obedience to the Father. In the upcoming sessions we will see what eternal significance Jesus's death has for us. Jesus is God. He is worthy of our worship and our praise. Just as the angels over Bethlehem praised God for Jesus's birth, one day all creation will bow at the name of Jesus and confess Him as Lord. (See Philippians 2:9–11.)

Jesus Came to Save: Sinners Are Lost and Need Rescue

Why would Jesus willingly leave all the glory of heaven and come to earth as a human? Jesus declared that He came *"to seek and to save that which was lost"* (Luke 19:10). Paul, a biblical writer and first-century missionary, marveled about Jesus's mercy in his letter to a young friend and co-worker named Timothy.

Find 1 Timothy 1:15–17 in your Bible or read it in the margin.

Paul remembers what his life was like before Jesus saved him. He was a Jewish leader (named "Saul" at the time) who would not accept Jesus as the Messiah. Paul greatly persecuted the first followers of Jesus. But Jesus sought Paul and saved him. (Read Acts 9:1–19 for the account of Paul's salvation.)

Q: Why did Paul say that Jesus came into the world?

- To save the sinners is everyone

> Here is a trustworthy saying that deserves full acceptance: Christ Jesus came into the world to save sinners—of whom I am the worst. But for that very reason I was shown mercy so that in me, the worst of sinners, Christ Jesus might display his unlimited patience as an example for those who would believe on him and receive eternal life. Now to the King eternal, immortal, invisible, the only God, be honor and glory for ever and ever. Amen.
> —1 Timothy 1:15–17

Q: What is the result of Christ's salvation in the life of an individual? (Also see John 17:3 to help with your answer.) *eternal life*

Paul's sins included imprisoning and executing Christians. God used Paul's life as an example to others that God can and will save anyone. No person is so sinful that God cannot save him or her. Paul allowed Jesus to rescue him and give him eternal life. How have you responded to Jesus's attempts to rescue you?

Open mind - present. - Being nicer to others
Closed mind - past - do things for others
with no expectations

Session Summary

Just like Paul, we are all sinners. We all break or ignore God's law and choose our own way. Therefore, we are lost, separated from God. Jesus came to earth to seek us or draw us to Himself and save us from the death our sin deserves. This was His earthly mission. He accomplished this by paying the penalty for our sin by dying on the Cross. Jesus's act of obedience makes our salvation possible by healing our broken relationship with God. *"Now this is eternal life: that they may know you, the only true God, and Jesus Christ, whom you have sent"* (John 17:3).

How do you receive this free gift of salvation? By admitting you are a sinner and cannot save yourself. By acknowledging that Jesus's death paid for your sins, and choosing to follow Jesus and turn your life over to Him. We will explore this more in upcoming sessions, but if God is asking you to respond to Him, do not wait. You can begin a relationship with God right now by committing your life to Him. You can express this commitment through a sincere and heartfelt prayer like the one below, though you should feel free to use your own words:

> *God, I believe You are the one true God and Creator of all things. I know that I am a sinner and deserve eternal separation from You. But, God, I believe Jesus died on the Cross to pay the penalty for my sin. I ask for Your forgiveness. I trust in You and want to live my life for You. Thank You for Your forgiveness and for eternal life with You. Amen.*

There is nothing magical in the words you pray. But if they truly reflect your heart's desire to follow Christ, trusting Him for new life now and forever, welcome to the kingdom of God! If you have prayed this prayer or a similar one for the first time, have questions, or need help, talk to a Christian friend or your Bible study leader.

Personal Story:
Pursued by God

God pursued Ron for 45 years.

Looking back, Ron can see God was reaching out to him in numerous ways, but he always ran away. "God was inviting me to know Him my whole life, but I refused to accept the invitation. When I finally understood God *wanted* a relationship with me I was overwhelmed."

Ron's mother and sister have both been Christians for many years. Ron always respected the faithfulness he witnessed in his mother's life, but could not understand the relationship she had with God. Ron considered his sister a Jesus freak. "Every time she tried to talk to me about Jesus I would escape," he admits. Yet, over the years they both continued to pray that one day Ron would stop running and turn to follow Jesus.

Although Ron believed in a greater power, some kind of divine being, he did not accept or understand the concept of a personal God with whom he could have a relationship. "I knew that we couldn't be all there is, but I didn't have a desire to learn more about God. If other people needed to go to church, then that was OK for them. But church wasn't for me. I thought the main purpose of attending church was to learn good values and morals."

Ironically, as a young man, Ron taught religion in a Catholic elementary school. But it was only a subject. Ron purposefully left God out of it. "I was teaching values and morals, not really about God." However, studying the Bible left an indelible mark on Ron.

Ron's misconceptions about church and faith kept him running. He thought church was just an organization that would try to force him to fit its mold. He didn't want any part of "church." The possibility of a relationship with God never entered his mind.

Then something happened that forced Ron to stop ignoring God's attempts to get his attention. Ron's teenage daughter, Courtney, became a Christian. She not only loved church, she asked her parents to go too. Ron and his wife Sandi agreed, but not because either of them wanted to attend. Their sole motivation was to support their daughter.

Almost immediately Sandi discovered her own desire to be in church and to learn as much about God as possible. Ron didn't feel the same spiritual urgency as his wife, but he was impacted by the friendliness of the people and the sense of family. After a while, Ron realized he wasn't attending church just to support Courtney. He genuinely liked being there.

Although Ron enjoyed the church experience, he continued to resist letting God have his life. He was independent; he did not need God. Then one day he was hit by the only truth that made a difference. *God* wanted a relationship with *Ron.*

Ron responded to this truth by trusting his life to Jesus. He doesn't run from God anymore. In fact, Ron spends his days following Him. (Read about Sandi, Ron's wife, in session 3.)

• •

Shepherds on a hillside outside of Bethlehem were the first to receive the angelic birth announcement. The Bible often uses the analogy of a shepherd and sheep for God and His people. Jesus called Himself the Great Shepherd. Jesus also tells a story about a shepherd and his sheep to describe how He seeks after lost people to rescue them.

Read Luke 15:3–7. Those originally listening to Jesus's story could easily identify with it. Sheep and shepherds were common everyday sights. Jesus knew all of his hearers would leave the group of 99 sheep to find the 1 that was lost.

Q: Can you think of times when you felt lost and in need of rescue? List some. *In the past many times - stood on my own 2 feet - Didn't know God.* *- KID - SKIN MY KNEES - LOOSE THINGS*

Q: Have you ever sensed God searching for you like the shepherd did the lost sheep? Make a list below of specific times. *2007 - tough year - that's when I started attending church -* *- FRIENDS CALLED ME A JERK - DURING TIME WITH EX - DID NOT FEEL LIKE ME - DID NOT KNOW*

Q: Even if you can't think of a specific time, the fact that you are *WHO I* involved in this study is evidence God is seeking you. The *WAS.* Bible says no one will come after Jesus unless God draws them (John 6:44). Pray and thank God for all the times He has sought after you. How do you think God wants you to respond to Him?

Jesus came to seek and to save the lost. This means He wants to heal our broken relationship with God that was caused by our sin. How is this possible? Is this accomplished through religious activities or church membership?

Next session we will see these things cannot mend the relationship and bring us salvation. We will meet a man named Nicodemus who came to see Jesus and asked Him how he could be saved. Read John 3:1–18 for Jesus's answer.

How Can I Be Saved?

*T*he summer my oldest daughter, Kelley, was nine years old, she decided she needed a new bicycle. The problem? Her birthday is in February; Christmas was far off; and she did not have any money. But with her goal in mind she determined to earn enough money to buy the bike of her dreams. She washed neighbors' cars, did extra chores around the house, and scooped doggy droppings from countless backyards. Two weeks later she had done it! With her purse on her shoulder we headed down to the store and returned with the object of her desires. She had wanted something and she had worked until she earned it. We were proud of her, and she was proud of herself.

Our society values achievement, success, and hard work. The old adage "You can't get something for nothing" is almost always true. It applies to every area of life. If you want a good job, you must educate yourself. If you want a loving spouse, you must win his or her heart. If you want to get ahead in life, you must work hard and save money.

But what about eternal life? In past sessions we learned that humanity's relationship with God has been broken because of sin. We also learned that Jesus, who *is* God, came to earth as a human to make a way for the break in our relationship to be mended. But how is this possible? What can we do to make things right?

In this session we're going to meet a man named Nicodemus who came to Jesus because he knew he was missing something. Nicodemus wanted to know how he could really be connected to God. Jesus's answer surprised Nicodemus because it was so different from what he and his culture expected. Jesus's answer may surprise you too.

❧ Religion Is Not Enough: You Must Be "Born Again"

It's true. You usually do get what you pay for. Generic canned goods and furniture that comes in a box prove the point. If you want the good stuff, it's going to cost you. But what about eternal life? What makes a person a Christian? And what exactly *is* a Christian anyway?

Q: What are some ideas people have about what it takes to be a Christian? *FAITH IN GOD - BELIEVE IN CHRIST DO GOOD THING BECAUSE OF GOD (JESUS) NOT FOR YOURSELF. BELIEVE WHAT JESUS DID & STOOD FOR*

> Now there was a man of the Pharisees named Nicodemus, a member of the Jewish ruling council. He came to Jesus at night and said, "Rabbi, we know you are a teacher who has come from God. For no one could perform the miraculous signs you are doing if God were not with him."
>
> In reply Jesus declared, "I tell you the truth, no one can see the kingdom of God unless he is born again."
>
> "How can a man be born when he is old?" Nicodemus asked. "Surely he cannot enter a second time into his mother's womb to be born!"
>
> —John 3:1–4

Find John 3:1–4 in your Bible or read it in the margin.

Nicodemus was a Pharisee. The Pharisees, one of the Jewish religious parties in the first century, believed that the way to God was through strict obedience to all the laws. Some of these laws came from God and some of these laws were added by men. This way of thinking is similar to many religions today.

Nicodemus was also a member of the Jewish ruling council called the Sanhedrin. The Sanhedrin was a 71-member council comprised of men from both main religious parties and presided over by the high priest. The Sanhedrin ruled Israel under the authority of the Roman government. Nicodemus was an important leader and a highly respected member of the community.

He recognized something great in Jesus. So one night Nicodemus managed to arrange an interview with this teacher, presumably hoping to find some answers to his burning questions.

Jesus seemed to know why Nicodemus came to see Him. By society's standards Nicodemus had it all together. If anybody had an "in" with God it would be Nicodemus. Yet he came to Jesus because he sensed Jesus could supply what he lacked.

Q: Based on Nicodemus's first statement (v. 2), what does he believe about Jesus? — *HE IS GODS SON*

Q: Based on Jesus's reply, what questions do you think were on Nicodemus's mind? *Didn't quite get the born again — relating to change in beliefs — how can I become born again. " " " teach others to be born again*

"The kingdom of God" refers to the time of God's reign and the place of His realm. To "see the kingdom of God" means that one is a part of God's kingdom and under His rule and authority. If you are in God's kingdom, then you are in a relationship with Him and have been given eternal life. This is what being a Christian means.

Jesus goes on to explain that a person becomes a member of His kingdom by being "born again." The word *again* in verse 3 is from the Greek word *anothen*, which has a double meaning. *Anothen* means "again" or "anew" and "from above," according to *The Complete Word Study New Testament*. To be "born again" means to be reborn spiritually. The Holy Spirit of God gives life to our spirit, which is dead because of sin. This happens by God's grace through a person's faith in the sacrificial death of Jesus. Nicodemus does not understand the meaning of Jesus's statement that you must be "born again" to be a part of God's kingdom, so Jesus goes on to explain.

Find John 3:5–8 in your Bible or read it in the margin.

Jesus describes a person's first or physical birth with the words *water* and *flesh*. Jesus also describes a second or new birth that brings us access to God. In this description He uses a play on words to teach something about the nature of God's Spirit. *The Complete Word Study New Testament* discusses the same Greek word, *pneuma*, which is translated as both "wind" and "Spirit" in verses 6–8. "Spirit" refers to the person of the Holy Spirit, who is the third person of the Trinity along with God the Father and God the Son (Jesus). (See "The Trinity," p. 76, for more information.)

> Jesus answered, "I tell you the truth, no one can enter the kingdom of God unless he is born of water and the Spirit. Flesh gives birth to flesh, but the Spirit gives birth to spirit. You should not be surprised at my saying, 'You must be born again.' The wind blows wherever it pleases. You hear its sound, but you cannot tell where it comes from or where it is going. So it is with everyone born of the Spirit."
> —John 3:5–8

Like the wind, we cannot see the Holy Spirit with our eyes, but we can see the effects of His presence. Jesus uses this analogy to describe the "new" birth.

Q: What effects of the wind's activity can be seen? What effects do you think can be seen when God's Spirit works in a person's life? - DESTRUCTION - LiFE - MOVEMENT BEAUTY

- HELPING-OTHERS - EFFECTS EVERYONE
- PEACE + HAPPINESS

Find John 3:9–18 in your Bible or read it in the margin.

Nicodemus was a religious leader and a teacher of God's Scripture. However, he did not really understand spiritual things and was not yet a part of God's spiritual kingdom. So, Jesus continued to explain the truth about salvation to him. In His explanation,

Jesus referred to Himself as the "Son of Man." This term was one Jesus used often and usually in association with His suffering and death. In this passage, Jesus referred to an incident recorded in the Old Testament in the Book of Numbers 21:4–9. He used it to portray what His upcoming death would accomplish. (Note: "The Son of Man must be lifted up" refers to Jesus being nailed to a wooden cross, being set vertically in a public place, and then left there to die.)

More than a thousand years earlier, when the Israelites were in the desert preparing to enter the Promised Land, they sinned against God by complaining about His provision for them. As a consequence of their sin, poisonous snakes came among them, killing many people. When their leader, Moses, prayed and asked God for mercy, God told Moses to make a snake of bronze and to put it on a pole. People who had been bitten could look at the snake and live. The Israelites who were bitten were under a penalty of death, but if they believed God's word and trusted in His promise by looking to the snake, God would give them physical healing.

"How can this be?" Nicodemus asked.

"You are Israel's teacher," said Jesus, "and do you not understand these things? I tell you the truth, we speak of what we know, and we testify to what we have seen, but still you people do not accept our testimony. I have spoken to you of earthly things and you do not believe; how then will you believe if I speak of heavenly things? No one has ever gone into heaven except the one who came from heaven—the Son of Man. Just as Moses lifted up the snake in the desert, so the Son of Man must be lifted up, that everyone who believes in him may have eternal life.

"For God so loved the world that he gave his one and only Son, that whoever believes in him shall not perish but have eternal life. For God did not send his Son into the world to condemn the world, but to save the world through him. Whoever believes in him is not condemned, but whoever does not believe stands condemned already because he has not believed in the name of God's one and only Son."

—John 3:9–18

This is a physical picture of a spiritual reality. Each of us has sinned and is under a penalty of spiritual death. But if we believe God's promise of spiritual healing and look to or trust in Jesus' sacrificial death to pay the penalty for our sin, God will give us eternal life.

Eternal life describes the change in our human existence that comes from placing faith in Jesus and His sacrifice. Our life is no longer defined by the physical (or own human will), but by the spiritual (or by the will of God). Eternal spiritual life begins as soon as we enter into a relationship with Jesus. The Bible says, *"Now this is eternal life: that they may know you, the only true God, and Jesus Christ, whom you have sent"* (John 17:3).

Q: Based on John 3:16–17 (see last paragraph of sidebar), why did God send His Son?

To save the people who believe in him. SAVE ETERNAL LIFE Is there only heaven + hell?

God's gift of His Son Jesus leaves every individual with a decision to make. There is no neutral ground when it comes to belief in Jesus Christ. All of us have sinned (Romans 3:23) and therefore deserve the death penalty (Romans 6:23). This is why John 3:18 says that whoever does not believe in Jesus and His payment for our sin stands condemned already. But those who believe are not condemned. Belief entails more than just acknowledgement. *The Complete Word Study New Testament* explains that the Greek word for this kind of belief is *pisteuo* and it includes the idea of entrusting or committing yourself to Jesus. Belief must be an active trust that leads to commitment and obedience. True spiritual rebirth is accompanied by this kind of belief.

The Trinity: Is God Three or One?

Christians are unique in their belief about the nature of God. Through Scripture we know there is only one God, who is Creator of all things. (See Isaiah 45:18.) However, also through Scripture, we learn that God is three persons: God the Father, God the Son, and God the Holy Spirit. (See 2 Corinthians 13:14.) God is three persons, yet one divine essence. The Trinity is a topic we have difficulty understanding. We must always see what the Bible says and then trust God with our limited understanding.

We Are Saved by Grace: Not by Good Things We Have Done

The New Testament Book of Titus further describes this spiritual rebirth. The Book of Titus is a letter from the missionary Paul to the young pastor Titus. Titus helped Paul on the island of Crete and was left behind to continue their work with the Christian churches there. Titus needed Paul's advice and guidance in leading the people.

Read Titus 3:3–7 in your Bible or in the margin.

Q: Underline words and phrases in the passage that describe the lives of Paul, Titus, and the people of Crete before meeting Jesus. List any similarities with your own life.

MANY THINGS

> At one time we too were <u>foolish, disobedient, deceived</u> and <u>enslaved by all kinds of passions and pleasures</u>. We lived in <u>malice</u> and envy, being <u>hated and hating</u> one another. But when the (kindness) and (love) of God our Savior appeared, he saved us, not because of righteous things we had done, but because of his (mercy). He saved us through the (washing of rebirth) and renewal by the Holy Spirit, whom he poured out on us (generously) through Jesus Christ our Savior, so that, having been justified by his (grace), [we might become heirs having the hope of (eternal life.)]
> —Titus 3:3–7

Q: Circle all the actions God took on their behalf. Put brackets around the results of God's actions.

Q: What characteristics of God's nature do you see in this passage?

- *MERCIFUL*
- *GRACEFUL*
- *LOVE*
- *KIND*

EVERYTHING CIRCLED

God is the same today as He was in the first century. The actions He took to rescue people then are the same actions He takes to save people today. We absolutely cannot save ourselves. But we can trust in God to save us.

Session Summary

A Christian is a person who is in a saving relationship with God through Jesus Christ. There is absolutely no good work or religious activity that anyone can do to earn the right to be a Christian. Church membership does not do it. Baptism does not do it. Church attendance or being a good person does not do it. Why? Because we can never be good enough.

From what are we saved? We are all sinners. Not one of us is able to live up to the image of God in which God created humanity. Our sin has broken our relationship with God and has brought with it the penalty of spiritual death, which is eternal separation from God.

How then can one be "saved?" Jesus told Nicodemus he must be *born again.* We must have a spiritual rebirth. Only God can accomplish this through the work of His Holy Spirit in us. This is possible through our belief in, and acceptance of, Jesus' sacrificial death on the Cross for us. God in His mercy and grace accepts Jesus's death as payment for our sin. With the penalty of our sin paid for, God washes us clean, and we are "born again" spiritually. If you have never been "born again," but are ready to have new life in Jesus Christ, don't wait. You can express your faith in Jesus right now in prayer. (See session summary in chapter 5, p. 66.)

Our salvation has nothing to do with us and everything to do with God. It is by His mercy and grace and the work of Jesus Christ that we are saved. This is at the heart of John 3:16, probably the best-known verse in the entire Bible: *"For God so loved the world that he gave his one and only Son, that whoever believes in him shall not perish but have eternal life."*

Personal Story:
Are You a Christian?

Greg always considered himself to be a Christian. He quickly answered yes when the pretty girl he was dating in college asked him if he was. But when he went to church with her one Sunday he discovered the truth.

Greg grew up believing in God. As a child, his parents took him to church several times a year. He even attended Sunday school occasionally. (But he didn't enjoy it at all.) Greg knew he wasn't Jewish or an atheist or a Muslim or any other "non-Christian" religion. The church he attended had the word "Christian" on the sign. Therefore, he had to be a Christian. It was a process of elimination.

However, Greg did not spend much time thinking about God. "I never thought about spiritual things. In retrospect, I was completely captivated with my own personal wants. As a boy I focused on my desires and how I could stay entertained. I was respectful toward God, but did not pursue a relationship with Him. But looking back I see that God pursued me. And I am so grateful."

During high school, God reached out to Greg through two little pamphlets someone left in his locker. The first explained how Jesus's death on the Cross provides forgiveness of sin and reconciliation with God. Greg read it about 10 times and then threw it away. About a month later a second pamphlet appeared in his locker. The topic was man's purpose in life. Greg was impacted by the truth that God the Creator had made him for a specific purpose. He read the pamphlet more than 30 times and never threw it away.

God used the pamphlets in Greg's high school locker to prepare his heart for the next divine encounter. In college, Greg met Lisa, a sweet beautiful young woman who loved Jesus. After they began to date, Lisa invited Greg to go to church with her. He never even considered telling her no.

During the service the minister talked about Jesus and how His sacrificial death on the Cross makes it possible for people to have a relationship with God. In fact, Greg learned that having a relationship with Jesus is what makes you a Christian. Going to church doesn't do it. Growing up in America doesn't do it. Calling yourself a Christian doesn't do it. Putting your faith in Jesus *does*. Greg realized he wasn't a Christian because he didn't have a relationship with Jesus.

That day, when Greg heard the truth about Christianity, it felt like an invitation straight from God. God was calling Greg to begin a personal relationship with Jesus. Immediately he answered yes to God and shared his decision with the minister. Greg knew the pamphlets someone left in his locker years earlier had prepared him to respond to God's urging to become a Christian.

Greg and Lisa married a few years later. Nearly 30 years and five children later Greg is still grateful that God pursued a relationship with him. They have sought to raise their children to know and love Jesus. And Greg always tries to remember that God created him for a purpose.

"God has a plan and purpose for my life. He wants me to live every day in a way that honors Him. He gave me faith so I could hear and respond to His call. I know He loves me and chose me to belong to Him. I want my life to please Him."

• •

✐◯ Find Out More ◯✎

During His earthly ministry Jesus often taught the crowds with parables. Parables are stories that use common, everyday subjects to teach a deeper meaning. In the 15th chapter of the Book of Luke, Jesus tells a parable about a father and his wayward son. The Bible often uses the relationship between a human father and his child to illustrate a spiritual truth about God and His relationship with us.

Q: Read Luke 15:11–32. Just like the father in this parable, God does not force anyone to be with Him. He created us with the freedom to choose because He wants us to choose Him. In the story, the younger son chose to leave his father and live his life his own way. Can you recall a time in your life when you consciously chose to live apart from God? If so, describe it.

MOST OF MY LIFE - BUMBLEING ALONG - NO FOCUS - NOT HAPPY

The young son had fun for a while. He spent money like it was going out of style. But pretty soon the money ran out. He began to feel the effects of famine and was forced to tend pigs, something he would have never pictured himself doing. For the Jew, pigs were unclean animals. By law they could not use them for sacrifices, eat them, or even touch them. This young man had hit bottom.

Q: Have you ever had to face unpleasant or even horrible consequences while living outside of God's will for you?

YES LAST MARRIAGE

Q: The Bible says when the young man *"came to his senses"* he hurried back to his father. He returned seeking forgiveness and restoration. How did his father respond? *HAPPYNESS FORGIVENESS*

Q: Based on this parable of Jesus, how do you think God responds when an individual returns to Him seeking forgiveness and restoration? *SAME*

How High
Is the Price?

*H*ave you ever owed a debt someone else paid for you? My friend Sue is a loving person who is always looking for ways to help others. Sue once loaned her car to friends while she was out of town. Several weeks later Sue received a surprise in the mail. It was a speeding ticket, given electronically by a camera snapping a photo of the license plate. It listed the location and date of the speeding incident. Sue racked her brain trying to remember driving down that particular street. Then the date jumped out at her. She hadn't even been in town on that date. Someone else—the borrowing friends—had been driving her car. Sue knew her friends could not afford the ticket as easily as she could. Sue paid the debt and never even told them about the ticket.

In the last session, we discovered we can't do anything to save ourselves from the death penalty our sin deserves. No amount of religious activity or good works can ever mend the broken relationship with God caused by our sin. Jesus told Nicodemus he must be "born again" spiritually to be a part of God's kingdom. But how is this possible?

Like the borrowing friends, our own actions have incurred a debt. We owe a debt we cannot pay ourselves. Our sin has incurred the death penalty. (See Romans 6:23.) But because He loves us, God came into the world to pay our debt Himself. This session we will see how Jesus Christ paid the debt we owe through His willing death on the Cross.

Jesus Took Our Place: He Put Himself in the Father's Hands

Jesus said He came to earth to seek and to save the spiritually lost. He knew how this would be accomplished. Jesus told His disciples He would be arrested, handed over to the Gentiles, mocked, flogged, and killed. But, He would also rise again. (See Luke 18:31–34.) The disciples, however, did not understand.

The night of His betrayal, Jesus spent intense time with His disciples trying to prepare them for what was ahead. Then when the time of His arrest drew near, Jesus went into the garden of Gethsemane to pray.

All four Gospels have a record of Jesus's betrayal, arrest, crucifixion, and death. We will look at pieces from each account.

Find Matthew 26:47–56 in your Bible or read it in the margin.

Earlier in the evening Jesus had predicted His betrayal. Although Jesus did not reveal the betrayer's name to the group, He knew it was Judas Iscariot, one of His 12 disciples. (See Matthew 26:20–25.) Judas had accepted 30 pieces of silver from the Jewish leaders in exchange for handing Jesus over to them.

While he was still speaking, Judas, one of the Twelve, arrived. With him was a large crowd armed with swords and clubs, sent from the chief priests and the elders of the people. Now the betrayer had arranged a signal with them: "The one I kiss is the man; arrest him." Going at once to Jesus, Judas said, "Greetings, Rabbi!" and kissed him.

Jesus replied, "Friend, do what you came for."

Then the men stepped forward, seized Jesus and arrested him. With that, one of Jesus' companions reached for his sword, drew it out and struck the servant of the high priest, cutting off his ear.

"Put your sword back in its place," Jesus said to him, "for all who draw the sword will die by the sword. Do you think I cannot call on my Father, and he will at once put at my disposal more than twelve legions of angels? But how then would the Scriptures be fulfilled that say it must happen in this way?"

At that time Jesus said to the crowd, "Am I leading a rebellion, that you have come out with swords and clubs to capture me? Every day I sat in the temple courts teaching, and you did not arrest me. But this has all taken place that the writings of the prophets might be fulfilled." Then all the disciples deserted him and fled.

—Matthew 26:47–56

Q: How did one of Jesus's disciples initially try to handle the situation? (In the Book of John we learn Peter was the one who wielded the sword. The Book of Luke records that Jesus healed the man's ear.)

FIGHTING – BRUTE FORCE – NO THOUGHT

Q: How did Jesus react to the situation? What did He say He could have done? Why did He not do this? *– TOLD ALL TO CALM DOWN – COULD HAVE USED GOD TO HELP BUT PROPHESIES WOULD NO BE FULFILLED*

Q: How did the disciples react when they discovered Jesus was not going to resist? *THEY RAN*

Find Mark 14:53–65 in your Bible or read it in the margin.

Earlier in Mark's Gospel we are told the Jewish leaders were looking for a way to get rid of Jesus because so many people were listening to Him and were amazed by Him. The leaders were worried they would lose some of their power and prestige. But because Jesus was so popular the leaders were afraid to arrest Him out in the open. So, they resorted to the pretense of justice under the cover of darkness.

> They took Jesus to the high priest, and all the chief priests, elders and teachers of the law came together. Peter followed him at a distance, right into the courtyard of the high priest. There he sat with the guards and warmed himself at the fire.
>
> The chief priests and the whole Sanhedrin were looking for evidence against Jesus so that they could put him to death, but they did not find any. Many testified falsely against him, but their statements did not agree.
>
> Then some stood up and gave this false testimony against him: "We heard him say, 'I will destroy this man-made temple and in three days will build another, not made by man.'" Yet even then their testimony did not agree.
>
> Then the high priest stood up before them and asked Jesus, "Are you not going to answer? What is this testimony that these men are bringing against you?" But Jesus remained silent and gave no answer.
>
> Again the high priest asked him, "Are you the Christ, the Son of the Blessed One?"
>
> "I am," said Jesus. "And you will see the Son of Man sitting at the right hand of the Mighty One and coming on the clouds of heaven."
>
> The high priest tore his clothes. "Why do we need any more witnesses?" he asked. "You have heard the blasphemy. What do you think?"
>
> They all condemned him as worthy of death. Then some began to spit at him; they blindfolded him, struck him with their fists, and said, "Prophesy!" And the guards took him and beat him.
>
> —Mark 14:53–65

Q: What kind of case did the Sanhedrin have against Jesus?

[handwritten: ∅]

False testimony was given, twisting a statement Jesus had made about the "temple." Jewish tradition held that when the Messiah came He would build a new temple. But the Old Testament Scripture (Zechariah 6:12–13) did not refer to an earthly temple, nor did Jesus Himself. The Bible tells us Jesus was referring to His body, which would die on the Cross but be raised to life three days later (John 2:19–20).

Q: Up to this point in the hearing Jesus had remained silent. Why do you think He did not defend Himself?

[handwritten: No REASON TO JESUS GOD KNEW THE ACCUSATIONS WERE FALSE]

Q: To what one question did Jesus respond? How did He respond?

[handwritten: Are you the son of God. YES - LOOK FOR ME IN THE FUTURE IN HEAVEN - BESIDE GOD]

Jesus's response claimed divine authority for Himself. He claimed to be God. The high priest tore his clothes in shock and mourning. By Jewish law, Jesus's claim of divinity was blasphemy and deserved death. However, it was not blasphemy if it was true.

Jesus Was Condemned: He Accepted Our Death Sentence

The Jewish leaders were limited in their authority by the Roman government. Because they could not administer the death penalty themselves, they had to take Jesus to Pilate, Roman governor of Judea from A.D. 26–36.

Find and read John 18:28–19:16 in your Bible. (Note: Entering a Gentile home would make a Jew ritually unclean and therefore unable to participate in the Passover and other Jewish feasts.)

Q: How would you describe the relationship between Pilate and the Jewish leaders?

[handwritten: SO-SO - JUST PUT UP WITH EACH OTHER]

Q: Apparently the Jewish leaders said Jesus claimed to be the king of the Jews in the charges they brought to Pilate. Why would they include this? What irony do you see here? ~ REJECTING GOD

*? - THE HIGH PRIEST IS HINTING HE IS KING OF JEWS - BUT KILLING - KING OF JEWS

Q: How did Jesus describe His kingship?

OF ANOTHER WORLD

Jesus told Pilate that His purpose was to reveal the truth. However, Pilate responded sarcastically with, *"What is truth?"* (John 18:38). Remember Jesus said, *"I am the way, the truth, and the life. No one comes to the Father except through me"* (John 14:6). How do you think Pilate would have responded if he knew the answer to his rhetorical question was in fact the person standing before him? ~ DID HE BELIEVE IN GOD"?

It was customary each year at Passover for Rome to release one Jewish prisoner. Even though Pilate did not understand who Jesus was, he did not believe Him to be guilty of anything deserving of death, so he called upon the custom in an attempt to release Jesus.

Q: When the Jews rejected Pilate's suggestion, what action did Pilate take as another attempt to appease them? How did they respond? ~ TO LET THEM DEAL WITH JESUS - No TALKED ABOUT THEIR LAWS - DON'T ALLOW THEM TO PUNISH -

The flogging Jesus endured at the hands of Roman soldiers was severe and life-threatening. The whip of leather thongs was probably fitted with sharp pieces of bone or metal. Stripped of His clothing, He would have been beaten until His flesh hung in bloody shreds. In mockery, the soldiers pressed a crown of thorns on His head and draped a purple robe across His shoulders. It was in this condition that Pilate once again presented Jesus to the Jewish leaders hoping they would be satisfied. Instead they insisted on the Crucifixion of the King of kings, and denied and rejected God. (See John 19:15.)

The first of the Ten Commandments God gave to Israel was *"You shall have no other gods before me"* (Exodus 20:3). Yet the Jewish leaders were so intent on getting rid of Jesus they compromised their allegiance to God their King. Caesar considered himself to be a "god," and the Jewish leaders claimed they had no king but Caesar. Their own words condemned them of blasphemy, all because they felt Jesus was a threat to their positions of power.

Both the Jewish leaders and the disciples misunderstood Jesus's purpose in coming. As we saw in His conversation with Pilate, Jesus's kingdom was to be a spiritual kingdom, not a physical one. Jesus did not come to be a political leader. He came to *"give his life as a ransom for many"* (Matthew 20:28). Jesus, once again comparing Himself to a shepherd, described His willingness to pay *our* sin debt in the passage below.

Find and read John 10:14–18 in your Bible.

Q: How far will Jesus, the good shepherd, go to protect His sheep? - SACRAFICE HIS LIFE

Q: Who has the power or authority to take the life of Jesus? ONLY HIMSELF - GOD-JESUS

Q: Keeping this truth in mind, consider Jesus's arrest, trial, and sentencing. Did God lose control of the circumstances? How did God work through the sinful actions of men to fulfill His purposes? NO - DRIVE HOME THE FACT BELIEVE IN JESUS - NOT OTHERS?

Session Summary

Jesus did not resist arrest. He remained silent during the course of false testimony. He endured humiliation and physical brutality.

With one word Jesus could have called an army of angels to free Him from His suffering. Yet He willingly submitted to the will of the Father. His obedience would provide the way of salvation for you and me. Next week we will further examine how Jesus's death paid the penalty for our sin and how His resurrection certifies His power to give us eternal life .

• •

Personal Story:
No Sin Too Big

He believed in God. He had been to church. His grand-parents modeled strong faith in Jesus. But Darrell chose to live his life his own way—without God.

His teenage years were filled with wild parties and dangerous stunts. Looking back, Darrell can't believe he lived through this rebellious period. Several times he nearly died because of his foolish behavior and poor choices.

One night in particular sticks in Darrell's mind. In the midst of a drinking binge Darrell climbed a 20-foot-tall diving board to impress his friends with his "fabulous" swan dive. On the second bounce the whiskey bottle fell from his pocket and smashed on the bottom of the pool. Darrell was so drunk he had not realized the pool was empty.

Feeling drawn to public service, Darrell spent six years in the military and more than 20 years in law enforcement. Unfortunately, his destructive and self-centered attitudes carried over into adulthood, so when Darrell was not on duty he pursued anything and everything that pleased him.

Because beautiful women and money pleased him, owning and operating a topless bar seemed like a great business venture. He and his partner spent many months doing research for the project. But before the bar opened, Darrell woke up to the seriousness of what he was doing. He backed out. Looking back he can't believe the way he tried to justify his immoral desires by telling himself he would be helping the dancers by providing them with benefits and child care.

Darrell's selfish behavior severely affected his personal life. By the time he was 40, he had three failed marriages.

Through all these experiences Darrell frequently thought about God. His desire to know God increased with every birthday. However, Darrell also realized he had not been living the kind of life that pleases God. He knew he did not deserve God's forgiveness. "I felt God would not forgive me for all the things I had done. As a result I continued on my path of destruction."

Then Darrell met a man who had the peace he had been longing for. Although this man had a past very similar to Darrell's, something had caused a radical change. The man gave all the credit to Jesus. His story gave Darrell hope. Maybe God could forgive him. Maybe God could change his life.

Not long after this encounter, a friend invited Darrell on a weekend church retreat. Now hopeful that he might find what he was looking for, Darrell accepted. During the weekend the truth of God's unconditional love and forgiveness washed over him for the first time since childhood. Now ready to accept God's grace, Darrell discovered what it meant to have a relationship with Jesus.

He found what he'd been looking for and more. Darrell found the peace that had eluded him his entire life. He found the forgiveness God freely offers through Jesus. And best of all, Darrell found God's unconditional love. "Everything you're not supposed to do I had done. But when I met Jesus all the junk in my life seemed insignificant. I wasn't immediately fixed, but I knew God could heal me."

Two years after Darrell gave his life to Jesus he married a fourth time. This time his marriage is different, because God is in charge. Both Darrell and his wife are living their lives following God. "My faith and relationship with Christ continues to grow, and I am ever amazed at God's mercy and love."

• •

☙ FIND OUT MORE ❧

Most of the Jewish people at the time did not understand Jesus's purpose on earth because they were consumed by their immediate situation. Their nation was not independent. They were ruled by the strong arm of Rome. They longed for independence. They hoped that when the Messiah came He would free them from their political oppressors and establish an earthly kingdom. Although God cares very much about our physical circumstances, our spiritual condition is His utmost priority. Jesus came to provide eternal, spiritual freedom for every person who would believe in Him.

Jesus's arrest, crucifixion, and death should not have been a surprise to God's chosen nation. The suffering of the Messiah for His people had been prophesied long before His coming. For example, about 750 years earlier God revealed His intentions through the prophet Isaiah.

Read Isaiah 53:1–12. In the space below write all the phrases that describe how the Messiah would pay the debt we owe. (See vv. 4–5.)

Q: How did we incur this debt? (See v. 6.)
We are all sinners

Q: Compare verse 7 to Jesus's behavior during His arrest and trials. What similarities do you see?
Quiet –

Q: List the things to which Jesus willingly submitted Himself for you and me. (See v. 12.) *Bore the burden of all our sins.*

Q: Think about what Jesus did for you. How do you think you should respond?

Isn't This Too Good to Be True?

*S*teel Magnolias is one of my favorite movies. (Spoiler alert: If you haven't seen the movie, skip to the next paragraph.) The main story line focuses on Shelby, a young diabetic woman played by Julia Roberts. Shelby and her new husband want to have a baby, but the doctors have warned against it as pregnancy could adversely affect Shelby's already fragile health. Sally Field, who plays the part of her mother, M'Lynn Eatenton, is shaken when Shelby becomes pregnant against the doctor's advice. Although Shelby gives birth to a healthy baby boy, the damage is done. Shelby's kidneys are failing. Although M'Lynn had been grieved with Shelby's choice to ignore the doctor, she lovingly gives her daughter one of her kidneys.

What's the biggest sacrifice you have ever made for someone else? I have made numerous little sacrifices for the ones I care about. There has even been a handful of what you might consider selfless acts. But my average level of selflessness is akin to giving up my place in line at the grocery store for someone with only a few items.

Would you give your life to save someone else? The Bible says it is rare, but possible, for someone to be willing to give his life for a good man. But Jesus went much further than that on our behalf.

He willingly gave His life to save you and me while we were still sinners. (See Romans 5:6–8.) His sacrificial death is what makes our salvation possible.

Jesus Paid Our Debt: His Death Was the Price

I find it so hard to comprehend Jesus's willingness to accept the death penalty you and I rightfully deserve. From the depths of His love and compassion, God provided payment for sins through the death of His own Son. There has never been a greater substitute or sacrifice.

Having endured a night without sleep and a severe flogging, Jesus was led away to be crucified. The condemned person was required to carry his own crossbeam to the place of crucifixion. This location was usually in a prominent public place. Once he arrived at the location, nails were driven through the person's wrists to the crossbeam, which was then lifted and affixed to the pole that was already standing upright. The body was given minimal support by a small wooden block on the pole to prevent the nails in the hands from tearing through. Finally, the feet were nailed to the post. Death was usually caused by loss of circulation, heart failure, and/or an inability to breathe.

Read Luke 23:26–56 in your Bible. As you read, fill in the table below.

Groups or Individuals	Their Actions and Responses to Jesus	Jesus's Response to Them
Jesus's followers	MOURNED + CRIED FOR HIM	-THINK ABOUT YOURSELF
The crowd	SAVE YOURSELF IF YOU ARE THE SON OF GOD	FORGIVE THEM THEY KNOW NOT WHAT THEY DO
The Jewish leaders	He stirs Things up makes trouble Crucify him	

-SAVE YOURSELF

GOD'S TRUTH REVEALED

Soldiers	MOCKED HIM BAVE YOURSELF IF YOU ARE KING OF JEWS	
First criminal	- SAVE YOURSELF + US	
Second criminal	TALKED HOW JESUS WAS UNJUSTLY CONVICTED	YOU WILL GO TO HEAVEN
The centurion	NEW JESUS WAS TRUE & GOOD	
Joseph	an CARED FOR - RESPECTFUL BURIAL FOR JESUS	

Q: Why do you think there were so many different kinds of responses to Jesus? Why do you think people respond differently to Jesus today? FEAR, INTEREST, FAITH IGNORANCE

Two unusual things happened as Jesus hung dying on the Cross. First, we are told the sun became dark from noon to three in the afternoon. (The ancient Jews began counting the hours of the day at sunrise, so the "sixth hour" in verse 44 was about noon.) As the King of the universe was dying, even creation seemed to grieve. Second, the curtain in the temple was torn in two. This curtain shielded access to the holy of holies in the Jewish temple. The very presence of God was believed to be in this small room. Only the high priest could enter the holy of holies and only once a year. That the curtain tore when Jesus died is significant. Jesus's death, which was payment for our sins, made it possible for us to have access to God. It opened the way for us to enter the holy of holies, the very presence of God. Hebrews 10:19–22 describes the access to God that Jesus's death made possible.

Sometime after Jesus took His last breath, the Roman soldiers pierced His side with a sword to confirm His death (John 19:33–34). Later, Joseph, a member of the Jewish ruling council, asked Pilate for Jesus's body. Joseph hastily wrapped the body and placed it in a tomb. The burial was rushed because the Sabbath began at sundown on Friday. Jewish law forbade certain activities on the Sabbath, which was the Jewish day of worship. Some of the women who had been following Jesus made plans to return to the tomb on Sunday morning to properly prepare His body.

Our Debt Is Canceled: The Blood of Jesus Buys Our Forgiveness

Sin brings death. Each of us deserves death because we are all sinners. That's why Jesus Christ's death is good news (or gospel) for every sinner. Jesus paid the penalty for our sin when He shed His blood and died on that Roman cross about 2,000 years ago. Jesus was able to pay our death penalty because He did not deserve it Himself.

The Bible says Jesus, the only person who never sinned, became sin for us so that we might take on His righteousness. (See 2 Corinthians 5:21.) We need the righteousness of Christ in order to have a relationship with God. *Righteousness* refers to an ability to conform to God's moral standard. No matter how good we are, we cannot be completely righteous. However, when we accept God's gift of grace by putting our faith in Jesus, Jesus takes our sin and gives us His righteousness.

Find Romans 3:21–25a in your Bible or read it in the margin.

> *But now God has shown us a way to be made right with him without keeping the requirements of the law, as was promised in the writings of Moses and the prophets long ago. We are made right with God by placing our faith in Jesus Christ. And this is true for everyone who believes, no matter who we are. For everyone has sinned; we all fall short of God's glorious standard. Yet God, with undeserved kindness, declares that we are righteous. He did this through Christ Jesus when he freed us from the penalty for our sins. For God presented Jesus as the sacrifice for sin. People are made right with God when they believe that Jesus sacrificed his life, shedding his blood.*
> —Romans 3:21–25 (NLT)

Q: After reading this passage, put in your own words why we need Jesus's righteousness, and how we can receive it. ⟶ *Frees us from our sins –* ⟶ *Believe in Jesus - who he was what he did for us.*

Q: How does verse 25 (see last paragraph of sidebar) describe Jesus's death on the Cross? What does this mean to you personally? *HE CHOSE TO SACRAFICE HIS LIFE. THANKFUL – KNOWING I MIGHT HAVE A CHANCE OF HEAVEN*

An Empty Tomb: Angels Announce Victory

Since Jesus's body was put in the tomb late in the day on Friday, the women who had faithfully followed Him had not had time to properly prepare His body. When they left the tomb on Friday they went home and prepared the burial spices in anticipation of their return to the tomb when the Sabbath ended on Sunday morning. (See Luke 23:56.)

Find and read Luke 24:1–12 in your Bible. Verse 2 tells us when the women arrived at the tomb they found the stone had been rolled away. Tombs of this type were usually caves whose openings were sealed by large, heavy boulders. These boulders were rolled downhill into place in a channel that had been cut for this purpose. It would have taken much more strength than that of a few women to move the stone. They had been worried about who would roll the stone away (Mark 16:3). The Bible tells us an angel rolled it away (Matthew 28:2). (Note: The men who "gleamed like lightning" in verse 4 are angels.)

Q: Besides an open tomb, what did the women find when they got there? *JESUS WAS NOT THERE*

Q: What did the angels encourage the women to remember?
The teachings (prophesy) of - JESUS → TO SINFUL MEN - crucified - then risen
Jesus had told His followers many times that He "must be delivered" into the hands of sinful men for crucifixion. They had not fully understood then, and, apparently, they still did not understand when it happened. Jesus's crucifixion and death were part of God's plan all along. His purposes had not been derailed.

Q: What has God said to you during this study that you need to remember and apply to your own life? Have you been obedient to what He said? *HAVE FAITH IN JESUS + WHAT HE DID (STOOD FOR) - LEAD A MORAL LIFE. TRYING.*

Q: What is the result of the women's report to Jesus's remaining 11 disciples (also called the apostles)?

DISBELIEF

Have you ever received news you had difficulty believing? It may have been because it was too good to be true or it may have been because it was so different from what you were expecting. The disciples had trouble believing the women's report. But it wouldn't be long before Jesus cleared things up. You can read more about the Resurrection in chapter 9.

Session Summary

Jesus' shed blood is the payment required for our own sin. The Bible says we are reconciled to God through Christ's death (Romans 5:10). His sacrifice makes it possible for you and me to be declared righteous and to enter into a relationship with God. We can now enter into His presence. The Resurrection confirms His power, authority, and victory; it is the stamp of approval on all He did and taught.

Salvation is a free gift from God. To receive this gift, we believe Jesus is the Son of God, put our faith in what He did on the Cross, and give our lives to Him as the resurrected Lord. As we will see in the next two sessions, this kind of faith will be active and obedient.

• •

Personal Story:
Experiencing God's Forgiveness

Chelsey used to think people who believed in God were stupid. She viewed them as weak, desperately clinging to myths to get through life. That was until *Chelsey* needed God.

Evolution and the big bang were the things Chelsey once believed in. Then life began to unravel. "God put my own foolishness to the test," she admits.

As a young adult, Chelsey got stuck in a destructive pattern of behavior. She cheated on Victor, the boyfriend she loved, and lost him. Chelsey's "friends" were a bunch of partyers whose goal was getting their next fix. Addiction was a natural consequence.

Chelsey describes this point in her life as "an empty, dark, and loveless place." With nowhere else to turn, she tried prayer. "I vaguely remember asking God—if He was real—to help me out of the awful pit I had dug for myself."

Somehow Chelsey managed to break the hold addiction had on her life. Chelsey began taking care of her health. Although physically better, she was lonely. The friends were gone. She deeply regretted her mistakes, especially the hurt she caused Victor. Chelsey still loved him but believed her sinful behavior had ruined any future they could have had together.

Looking back, Chelsey realizes the things that happened next were the result of God's grace and activity in her life. Victor called. After a few cautious months of rebuilding broken trust, Victor and Chelsey began a life together.

They bought their first house when Chelsey became pregnant and then married soon after their son, Arrie, was born. Their new neighbors, Dan and Amber, were a friendly young couple with small children. When they all had dinner together, Chelsey discovered Dan and Amber were in her words, "Bible thumpers." But that didn't discourage her from building a friendship with them. "They were the kind of friends I had been looking for—fun, loving, family-oriented—and no partying."

Not long after Arrie was born, Amber invited Chelsey to go to a Bible study for young moms. Chelsey had been thinking a lot about what she wanted for Arrie. "Victor and I really wanted to be good parents, to raise him in a loving home. Going to church sounded appealing to me. I thought it could help us be 'good' parents."

During the first few weeks of the Bible study, Chelsey wanted to believe in God but was skeptical. "I remember thinking if God were real this would be great, this would really work. But I struggled to believe the Bible was really from God and not just made up by man."

Another hurdle was to believe Jesus would pay the penalty for her sins. Chelsey thought her sins were too big. But God was working in Chelsey's heart and mind. She was open to the truth and God made it clear to her. The more Chelsey got to know God, the more she understood how much He loves her. Before the Bible study ended after several weeks, Chelsey came to trust Jesus. He became her Savior.

Chelsey recalls the moment of her salvation with deep gratitude. "I did not deserve God's forgiveness. The damage my sin caused remained, but to be forgiven took a huge burden off my shoulders. It was a humbling experience. Words cannot describe the effect God's grace has had on me. I am so thankful to have Jesus in my life."

God's grace miraculously touched another relationship in Chelsey's life. She had not seen her mother in more than five years. Her mother's life choices had caused deep hurt in Chelsey's life. Chelsey had even refused for her to see Arrie. "God made it clear He wanted me to forgive my mom. I didn't want to, but Jesus changed my heart. God expressed His love and forgiveness to my mother through me," Chelsey explains.

The relationship was not healed overnight. Chelsey called it a "process of faith," as God lovingly led her in one step of obedience after another. Now, Chelsey's mom lives near them. She not only has a strong relationship with the entire family, she also has a new relationship with Jesus. "God not only changed my heart, He changed my mom's life too." (Read about Victor, Chelsey's husband, in session 1.)

• •

༄ࢺ Find Out More ࢺ༄

Read Colossians 1:15–23. Only God can save us from spiritual death. Verses 15 and 19 remind us that Jesus is fully God. Jesus's purpose on earth was to make our salvation possible. Jesus is able to save because He is God.

Q: List all the characteristics of Jesus found in verses 15–19 that show He is God.

Q: What is a person's condition before he or she is saved by Jesus?

Q: What are the results in a person's life after he or she accepts the gift of salvation that comes through faith in the work of the blood of Jesus? List all you can find.

Q: The last phrase of verse 22 is a good description for the word *righteous*. How is it described?

Q: Do you desire to be near to God, in His presence? If so, express your desire by writing a prayer to God below.

Is There Hope for My Future?

*P*roblems arose during the birth of our first child, Kelley. During the delivery, Kelley went into fetal distress. The doctor quickly delivered her with forceps. My husband, Wayne, and I began to rejoice when the doctor said, "It's a girl." But when we didn't hear her cry we began to understand something was wrong. Kelley was not breathing; she was blue all over. The doctor and nurses began to work over her furiously. They gave her oxygen but she still did not breathe on her own. Wayne and I were scared and confused about what was going on. After a couple of minutes when they still could not get Kelley to breathe, they brought in a small pair of shock paddles. As they prepared to shock our small daughter's heart, she began to breathe. Our fear turned once again to joy and then to gratitude when we learned she was completely healthy.

What happened with Kelley's delivery was certainly not what we had expected. Had the crisis ended in the loss of our baby, our future would have been very different.

Jesus's followers had not expected His death. Their hopes and dreams for what Jesus would do were buried in the tomb with His body. After His death they huddled together in grief and fear. Their future was bleak. They did not understand that He had come to die and what His death had accomplished for them. They did not understand it was all God's plan from the beginning. They certainly did not anticipate what happened next. In this session, we will continue considering the Resurrection, how Jesus defeated death by rising from the dead. We will also discover the significance His resurrection has for us today and eternally.

Jesus Is Alive: Death Could Not Hold Him

The angels announced it. The women carried the message of victory over death to Jesus's disciples. Was Jesus really alive? Was there still hope of a future with Jesus?

Find and read Luke 24:36–49 in your Bible.

The women were not the only ones who brought news of Jesus's resurrection to the disciples. Two of Jesus's followers also came to them with a report they had seen Jesus and talked with Him. While they were discussing this with the disciples, Jesus appeared in the room with them. The disciples were afraid and misunderstood the nature of His resurrection. They thought He was merely a spirit or they were somehow being deceived.

Q: How did Jesus attempt to erase their doubts?

Jesus went on to tell them what had to happen next. His crucifixion and resurrection were not the end, but a new beginning. Now His followers had to tell others how they could know Jesus. A relationship with Jesus begins with repentance. Jesus's death made it possible for our sins to be forgiven so we can be reconciled to God. But to receive God's forgiveness for our sins we must repent. Repentance means we must admit we are sinners, turn from our own way, and turn to God's way.

The Bible tells us that Jesus called for repentance and belief from the very beginning of His ministry on earth (Mark 1:14–15). An active belief in who Jesus is and what He accomplished for us on the Cross and repentance from sin makes it possible for us to become citizens of His spiritual kingdom.

Look back at Luke 24:49. Here, Jesus reminded the disciples about one of His promises. This promise is for those who come into a relationship with Him, those who belong to His kingdom. This is the promise of the presence of the Spirit of God, or the Holy Spirit, in the lives of Christians. If you have a true relationship with Jesus, then you have His Spirit. (Please see the inset below for more information on the Holy Spirit.)

Understanding the Holy Spirit

- *He is God.* The Bible teaches that God is three distinct persons in one unified nature. *Trinity* is the term used to describe our three-in-one God. (See Mark 1:9–11 for an example.) The Holy Spirit is eternal. He was present and active at Creation. (See Genesis 1:2.)

- The word *Trinity* is not found in the Bible. The word was coined by Christians years later to describe the nature of God as portrayed in Scripture. So, while it is not a biblical term, it is a term clearly based on the Bible's authoritative message.

- *He is God, present with Christians.* The Holy Spirit fills a person the moment he or she chooses in faith to trust Jesus with his or her life. (See Ephesians 1:13.) The Holy Spirit is the very presence of God in the life of a believer. (See John 14:16–18.)

- *He is our proof and guarantee.* The presence of the Holy Spirit in the life of a believer is proof he or she truly belongs to God. He is also God's guarantee that we will receive the spiritual inheritance God has promised us. (See 2 Corinthians 1:21–22.)

- *He is God's conforming power.* When believers yield their lives to the activity of the Holy Spirit He is able to shape their character to conform to Christ's. (See Galatians 5:16–22.)

- *He is our helper*. Among other things, the Bible calls the Holy Spirit our Counselor, Comforter, and Teacher. He helps us live the life God wants us to live. (See Romans 8:5–11.) He also helps us pray. (See Romans 8:26–27.)

The disciples were only a few of many who saw the resurrected Christ. The Bible records several of these post-resurrection appearances. These and others are summarized in the following Scripture passage.

Read 1 Corinthians 15:3–8 in the margin.

Q: Circle all the individuals and groups of people Jesus appeared to after His resurrection.

Q: Is it significant to you that the resurrected Christ appeared to so many people? Why?

For what I received I passed on to you as of first importance: that Christ died for our sins according to the Scriptures, that he was buried, that he was raised on the third day according to the Scriptures, and that he appeared to Peter, and then to the Twelve. After that, he appeared to more than five hundred of the brothers at the same time, most of whom are still living, though some have fallen asleep. Then he appeared to James, then to all the apostles, and last of all he appeared to me also, as to one abnormally born.
—1 Corinthians 15:3–8

The Resurrection is God's proof that everything Jesus said and did is true. It is also evidence that His death was an acceptable sacrifice for our sins. The early followers were convinced. After Jesus's death they were disillusioned and fearful, but after the Resurrection they became bold and courageous. They immediately began to turn the world upside down with the story of Jesus. It wasn't even just because they had faith that Jesus was alive. They knew Jesus was alive because they had seen Him with their own eyes.

It strengthens my own faith to think about the fact that these who walked with Jesus on earth were more willing to die than to recant the story of Jesus and His resurrection. They would not die for something they knew to be false. Therefore it must be true. And because Jesus is alive today I can have hope in a future with Him.

Martyrs for Jesus

Many of Jesus's followers were killed because they refused to recant the Resurrection and their faith in Him. They were so convinced it was true they would rather die than reject Jesus. Here are just a few of their stories based on Herbert Lockyer's *All the Apostles of the Bible,* which I recommend if you would like to read more about the sufferings of these giants of our faith.

- Andrew—An account from the fourth century reports his death by crucifixion in A.D. 60 in Greece. According-ing to tradition, he was killed because his testimony about Jesus converted the governor's wife.

- James, Son of Zebedee—The first of the apostles to be martyred. King Herod had him put to death with the sword. (See Acts 12:2.)

- James, Jesus's younger brother—Tradition says he was thrown from a pinnacle of the temple in A.D. 62 by Jewish leaders. Surviving the fall, he was then beaten until he died.

- Matthew—Tradition indicates he was killed by the sword in Ethiopia.

- Matthias (took Judas's place)—He was stoned and then beheaded around A.D. 64.

- Peter—According to church tradition, he was crucified upside down in Rome and his wife was martyred along with him.

- Philip — He was whipped, scourged, and then hung in Phrygia.

- Thomas — A tradition says he was killed in India by a lance through his body while kneeling in prayer.

Jesus Is the Resurrection and the Life: Do You Believe This?

Why must we believe in Jesus and His death and resurrection? To gain some insight, let's back up for a moment and take a look at an encounter that took place a little while before Jesus's arrest. One of Jesus's friends, a man named Lazarus, had died. Jesus went to see Lazarus' sisters who were also His friends. Martha ran out to meet Jesus on the road as He was arriving.

Find and read John 11:21–27 in your Bible.

Q: What did Martha's statement in verses 21–22 reveal she believed about Jesus?

Jesus took advantage of this moment to teach Martha something of vital importance about Himself. *Resurrection* refers to the biblical teaching that at the end of this physical age, when Jesus returns, He will completely and physically restore believers to life. Because Jesus was resurrected from the dead, He has the power to restore all who believe in Him — both spiritually and physically. The Bible teaches that when Jesus comes again to earth, all who belong to Him will receive a special glorified body. (See Philippians 3:20–21.)

Q: Restate Jesus's response in John 11:25–26 in your own words.

Q: Jesus asked Martha if she believed this. Do you believe this?

____Yes   ____No   ____Not sure

Belief in Jesus affects both our current life, our physical death, and our eternal destiny. Those who believe in Jesus receive power from Him through the presence of the Holy Spirit. We can live our lives in this world because He is Life. Also, physical death has no lasting power over believers because Jesus is the Resurrection. Our eternal future is determined by faith in Christ. Jesus broke the hold and sting of physical death by His resurrection. Because the grave was not the final reality for Jesus, death is not the final reality for those who put their trust in Him.

What Does It All Mean?

The purpose of this study is to present the truth about Jesus and give each participant the opportunity to respond to God. The following is a recap (an extended session summary) of what we have learned so far from the Bible.

- God is real and makes Himself known to mankind through the Bible and through Jesus Christ, who is the only way to God. (See John 14:6.)

- God created everything that exists, including you. He has the right of ownership to everything, including you. (See Psalm 24:1–2.)

- God created you in His image. You were made to worship God and have joy and peace in relationship with Him. This relationship defines the meaning and purpose intended for your life. God's ultimate purpose for you is to be like Jesus. (See Romans 8:29.)

- But your sin has broken your relationship with God and has earned you the penalty of eternal spiritual death and separation from God. (See Romans 3:23 and 6:23.)

- Because God loves you and is merciful, He desires to restore the broken relationship. Therefore, Jesus, who is God, came to earth to make a way possible for us to be saved from death. (See John 3:16.)

- There is no way that you can save yourself. No amount of good works or religious activities can accomplish this. The only way to be saved is by being spiritually born again. (See John 3:5.)

- Jesus Christ, who was completely sinless, willingly gave His life on the Cross to pay the penalty for your sins. Because He took your sin, you can receive His righteousness. (See 2 Corinthians 5:21.) This is a free gift of God. However, we must accept this gift. (See Romans 3:23–25.)

- Jesus's resurrection breaks the hold of physical death and gives you the hope of an eternal future with Him. (See John 11:25–26.)

How Should I Respond?

Sin has broken your relationship with God, and you are condemned to eternal death. But because He loves you, God sent Jesus to pay the penalty of your sins by His death on the Cross. Jesus's crucifixion and resurrection make a way for you to have a relationship with God now and to live eternally with Him. This eternal life is a free gift of God's grace. However, it does not come to every person automatically.

You must accept God's free gift. But how do you do this?

- You must admit you are a sinner. You must confess this to God and repent, turning from your sin to God. (See Acts 3:19.)

- You must believe that Jesus is God's Son and trust Him as the Savior that paid for your sins on the Cross. (See John 20:31.)

- You must believe that Jesus was resurrected and confess Him as Lord of your life. (See Romans 10:9–10.)

To *believe* in Jesus means you put your faith, or trust, in Him. Believing in Jesus is more than just intellectual acknowledgment. It means turning your life over to His control.

Making Jesus your Lord means that you give up running your own life for your own purposes. (See Galatians 2:20.) It means that just as Jesus died on the Cross, you willingly "die" or give up any rights to your own life. The Holy Spirit comes into your life, giving you spiritual rebirth. You die to your self-centered values and practices and receive a new identity in Christ. You turn your life over to Christ and let Him have control, not just intellectually, but with your whole heart. You allow Him to reshape your life and your identity. Jesus now has control of your life, living out His purposes through you. His purposes for your new life include good works as you obediently follow His direction. (See Ephesians 2:10.)

This is what it means to be a Christian. Your spirit, once dead in sin, has been brought back to life by the blood of Christ. Have you accepted this gift and given your life to Him? If not, why not?

If you desire to become a Christian—to commit your life to Christ—you can do that right now. Just express your repentance and commitment to God through a simple heartfelt prayer of faith. Your new relationship with Jesus makes you a Christian—the prayer does not. The prayer is merely a reflection of what's in your heart and mind. If you have questions or need help, talk to your study leader.

• •

Personal Story:
The Spirit Led Her

Karen had left God in her childhood. But she carried the hurt and pain of abuse and abandonment into her adult years. Although ambivalent toward God, Karen considered herself "spiritual" and dabbled in things like astrology.

Following her husband into what seemed like an "innocent" adventure, Karen spent more than a decade living in a nudist community. In reality, she was caught in an immoral lifestyle that didn't include God. Karen now describes those days as "very dark." But in the middle of this darkness, God revealed His light.

An acquaintance invited Karen to a Bible study. She agreed, thinking it would be an "interesting activity" and an "intellectual challenge." Karen also began to read the Bible on her own. "It began to make sense to me in a way I never understood before." Soon she was reading as much as she could, devouring every word. From the Bible, Karen learned what it means to be a Christian.

One day, Karen obeyed what she knew God had been leading her to do. She surrendered her life to Jesus, receiving Him as Savior and Lord. "I *knew* my life was different, that something significant had happened. I encountered such a sense of warmth, love, and acceptance from God."

Karen credits the Holy Spirit for accomplishing what God wanted for her life. The Spirit, and no one else, led her to Christ. The Spirit convicted her of sin and led her to make radical changes. Wearing clothes and burning her astrology books were among the first steps. The Spirit was also Karen's teacher as she read the Bible and learned about God.

The people in her world noticed immediately. "The nudist community responded with animosity and hostility," Karen says. Karen suffered a variety of daily challenges, including verbal abuse and hate mail.

The change also disrupted her marriage. Because Karen's husband, Rod, was the primary leader of the nudist club and owned the campground where they all lived, he received tremendous pressure from the members to do something about his wife. Initially Rod tried to logically prove to Karen there was no conflict between Christianity and nudism, but God had already shown her the opposite was true.

Karen's faith became a huge threat to their way of life because Rod was so dedicated to the nudist movement. So when logic did not work his resistance progressed to insults and put-downs. Rod called Karen "brainwashed" and claimed her faith was an "addiction to God." The tension in their marriage lasted for years.

With no other Christians in the nudist community, Karen was forced to depend on God. She sought God's guidance and strength to navigate the environment in which she felt trapped. He provided grace and protection to keep Karen growing spiritually in the midst of tremendous pressure.

She couldn't stay out of the Bible. "Being in God's Word felt as natural as breathing." Karen spent hours at a time searching the Scriptures to learn about God and her new faith. God Himself was her teacher.

In the early days of her faith Karen learned to depend on the Holy Spirit and to be alert to His guidance. She had to cling to the only light in the darkness. "I was wearing the armor of God every day—along with clothes! I tangibly felt God with me in those days like none other. The world I was in was very dark."

Four years after Karen became a Christian, the nudist club left their property. The financial situation of the club had become so bad Rod was forced to convert it to a regular campground. "God began to work in our circumstances so the way would be clear to work in Rod's heart."

One week after the nudist club left their property, Rod gave his life to Jesus. He now understood the changes that had taken place in Karen. Over time, their marriage healed as Rod got to know Jesus better. Even the campground—which was once a dark place—flourished as a family getaway. God not only saved Karen, He also filled her life with light.

• •

Read Romans 6:1–14. In his letter to the Christians in Rome the Apostle Paul explains salvation. These verses give a wonderful picture of what our new life in Christ means and what it should look like.

Q: In what ways does becoming a Christian resemble the death and resurrection of Jesus?

Q: What do the Crucifixion and Resurrection accomplish for us?

Q: What should our new life in Christ look like?

Verses 3 and 4 specifically refer to Christian baptism. Baptism by immersion in water is a picture or symbol of what Jesus has done in the life of a Christian. When a Christian is baptized, it is a witness to everyone she has accepted God's free gift of salvation and has given her life to Jesus. Even Jesus was baptized in obedience to the Father. Believers should follow the example of Jesus and be baptized as a testimony to the new life they have in Jesus. We will explore this more in session 10.

What Now?

My husband and I were married in 1983. The wedding ceremony was only the beginning of our marriage relationship. Although we had dated and even made plans for a future together, real commitment did not happen until we said, "I do." That was also the point where we began to really get to know each other. It hasn't always been easy. In fact, there have been times when one or both of us felt like walking away. But every time, we both chose to remain faithful to our commitment to each other.

Intimacy in a relationship takes time and hard work. It comes from talking, listening, spending time together, and sharing all the small and big things of life. Wayne and I know each other significantly better than we did in 1983. In fact, not long ago, Wayne and I were playing a game with friends in which the players make up definitions to little known words. Then everyone has to guess which one is the real definition. In one round, when the phony definitions were read there were two that were almost word-for-word the same. Wayne and I had made up the exact same thing. I guess after spending a lot of time together over the years, we have even begun to think alike!

Last session you were challenged to commit your life to Jesus. If you made this decision, you may be wondering, "So, what do I do now?" The Bible says, *"Now this is eternal life: that they may know you, the only true God, and Jesus Christ, whom you have sent"* (John 17:3). Your new life as a Christian, first and foremost, involves getting to know Jesus. As you spend time with Him and begin to follow Him, He will guide your life.

Difficult times may come when you will feel like walking away. But remember, God will never walk away from you. Commit to the time it takes to get to know Jesus. You will learn to trust Him and His direction for your life. Like Wayne and me, who have begun to think alike, you will find that as you spend regular time with Jesus you will begin to think like Him and adjust your life to His.

This session we will look at what the very first Christians did when they decided to give their lives to Jesus. They committed to a relationship to God and to each other. What the Christian life looked like then is what the Christian life should look like today.

Jesus Returned to Heaven: He Sent Us the Holy Spirit

The Book of Acts is a historical account of the beginnings of Christianity—how it started and how it grew. Acts also describes how the first Christians functioned as part of a community of Christians. It tells us a lot about how they lived out their new lives in Christ. Studying Acts can help new Christians today know how to be faithful followers of Jesus and members of a loving group of Christ followers.

Jesus Himself helped the first group of Christians get started on their journey of faith. He spent forty days physically among them after His resurrection before returning to heaven.

Find and read Acts 1:1–11 in your Bible.

Q: What did Jesus do during the 40 days between His resurrection and ascension to lay a good foundation for His followers?

The disciples' question to Jesus in Acts 1:6 reveals they still did not completely understand or know everything about their new faith. They were still confusing earthly and temporal matters with spiritual and eternal things. This should be encouraging to new Christians today. It takes time to learn and grow in your faith. So be patient! And Jesus does not leave His followers—then or now—to stumble along on their own.

In the last session, we read about Jesus's promise of the Holy Spirit. (See Luke 24:49.) Jesus repeated the promise here in the first chapter of Acts. The promise was fulfilled about ten days later on the day of Pentecost. Acts 2:1–4 tells us each believer received the Spirit. Although Jesus had physically returned to heaven He sent the Holy Spirit to be with believers in His place.

Q: If you have yielded your life to Jesus, the Holy Spirit is a constant presence in your life. In what ways are you experiencing His presence?

Look back at Acts 1:8. Jesus tells us the Holy Spirit gives us power to carry out God's direction for our lives. This passage contains a direction from God that applies to all believers. It is known as the Great Commission. This directive is for all of God's people, not just the first-century disciples/apostles. Jesus's last command should be our first concern.

Q: The apostles were eyewitnesses to Jesus and what He did for all of us. But we are witnesses, too. What personal experience do you have with Jesus you can share with others?

After giving His last instructions, Jesus ascended into heaven. Standing on the Mount of Olives, outside of Jerusalem, the believers watched Him go. Even after Jesus's sandals disappeared in the clouds they continued to stand there, gaping at the sky. I wonder how long they would have stood there had two angels not shown up.

Q: These angels gave the believers another promise. What was it?

Jesus is coming again! Jesus said He was leaving to prepare a place for us and that He will be coming back to take us to be with Him. (See John 14:2–3.) Because Jesus rose from the dead we can be assured that He can and will fulfill this promise to us. Until then He is present with us by His Holy Spirit.

The angels' statement reminded the apostles (*apostle* means one sent on a mission) that until Jesus returned there was work to be done. However, they needed the powerful presence of the Holy Spirit to carry out Jesus's mission. So they hurried back to Jerusalem to wait for His arrival.

The Church Begins: You Have a Place

After the believers received the Holy Spirit, God immediately used them to tell others about Jesus. Pentecost, held 50 days after Passover, was an annual festival to celebrate the harvest. Because it was a major celebration, Jews living in many other nations gathered in Jerusalem to observe it. On the day of Pentecost, the Apostle Peter preached his first sermon. Peter told the crowd that had gathered about Jesus. He described His death and resurrection and proclaimed that Jesus is both Lord and the promised Messiah.

Read Acts 2:36–47 to see what happened. The crowd responded immediately to Peter's call to repent. Three thousand people accepted his message that day and were baptized. Many of these pilgrims from other countries then returned to their own homes taking the news of Jesus with them.

Baptism is one of two *ordinances* (symbolic acts) Jesus instituted for His followers. Both ordinances—baptism and the Lord's Supper—are physical illustrations that remind Christians of Jesus' sacrifice. Understood in light of the teaching of the entire New Testament, baptism is an outward sign of what has already taken place in a believer's heart. The act of baptism is a witness to others of the commitment a believer has made to Jesus.

Baptism was just the first step for the 3,000 brand-new Christians. Acts 2 also records other activities to which the new believers were committed.

Q: List the four things in verse 42 to which the new believers were "devoted" or faithfully practiced.

The teaching of the apostles was the first thing to which the new believers were devoted. The apostles taught from the Old Testament Scriptures and from the teachings of Jesus. Today this is all together in our Bible. It is vital for all Christians, new and not so new, to spend time reading and studying God's Word.

Second Timothy 3:16–17, which we read in our first session, describes how God's Word should be used in our lives. *"All Scripture is God-breathed and is useful for teaching, rebuking, correcting, and training in righteousness, so that the man of God may be thoroughly equipped for every good work."*

Q: What do you think this could look like in your own life?

The second thing to which the new believers were devoted was the fellowship. The Greek word translated "fellowship" is *koinonia.*

Ajith Fernando's study aid *The NIV Application Commentary: Acts* defines *koinonia* as fellowship, intimacy, and a unique sharing. This refers to both the relationship a believer has with God and with other believers. Just as God created Adam and Eve to be in relationship with God and each other, God intends for every Christian today to live in relationship with Him and other Christians.

The way *fellowship* is used in verse 42 means that the new believers spent time together in a group. The Bible calls this community of believers the "church." The Bible also calls the church the body of Christ. Jesus is the head and His followers are the body.

Read 1 Corinthians 12:12–18, 25–27.

Q: After reading this passage, how would you describe what "church" is?

Q: As a believer, what place do you feel church should have in *your life?*

Each part of the human body is needed for it to operate like God intended. It is the same with the spiritual body, the church. When God saved you, He saved you *into* the body of Christ. No Christian can live the life God intends for her outside a local church. When we are born again we are born into a community of believers. God designed it this way for our mutual benefit.

A few years ago, we got news that Wayne's mother was killed in a car accident. Within a half hour our home was filled with dear friends from our church. They came to pray, offer practical assistance, and grieve with us. Because we had to prepare to travel immediately, there was much to do. Our Christian brothers and sisters quickly took on one responsibility after another. God directly cared for us through His church.

After teaching and fellowship, the third thing to which the new believers devoted themselves was the breaking of bread. This refers to the second ordinance of the church, which Jesus established with His followers the night He was arrested. (See Luke 22:7–23.) This ordinance is called the *Lord's Supper*. It is a proclamation of the Lord Jesus's death—the sacrifice that makes our salvation possible. This observance touches the heart of the Christian faith.

Read 1 Corinthians 11:23–26. (This passage describes the very first time this act was observed.)

Q: Why do you think the Lord's Supper is important for Christians to observe?

The fourth thing the believers devoted themselves to was prayer. Prayer is simply conversation with God. It is two-way. We do not merely talk to God; we must also listen to God.

The Bible clearly tells us we should *"pray continually"* (1 Thessalonians 5:17). A believer should have a constant attitude of prayer. This means he or she is always aware of God and ready to pray consciously at any time. Prayer and Bible reading go together as the best way to establish and maintain an open line of communication with God. This is how we get to know Him. Because prayer and Bible reading establish our vital link with God, we will explore them more in session 11.

Acts 2:43–47 gives us further information about the first church. God confirmed the apostles' authority in the church by doing miracles through them. The members of the church helped each other when physical needs arose. The first church was a close, intimate community. God worked through His community to care for and show love to each of His followers. This was not some group-enforced communism. But they did help each other, freely and without reservation, when help was needed. (Note: The phrase, "broke bread," in v. 46 is a slightly different grammatical composition than v. 42. Here it refers to hospitality, friendship, and socializing.)

As we have seen, God saves us, by His grace, through our faith in Jesus. There is nothing we can do to save ourselves. However, when God does save us, He expects us to be obedient to His direction through the Holy Spirit in our lives. This obedience will result in good works. (See Ephesians 2:8–10.) As we are obedient, God will use us to care for other believers and to reach out to the world around us.

Session Summary

If you have given yourself to Jesus and made a commitment to follow Him, then you are a Christian. We can learn about how a Christian should live today by studying how the first Christians followed Jesus in the Book of Acts. This is what we discovered:

1. The first Christians were baptized in obedience to Jesus's example and as a testimony to their new life.
2. The first Christians received the Holy Spirit to empower and guide their lives.
3. The first Christians listened to and studied God's Word.
4. The first Christians were part of a local church or community of believers.
5. The first Christians observed the ordinance of the Lord's Supper.
6. The first Christians devoted themselves to prayer.
7. The first Christians obeyed God's direction, which resulted in helping their fellow Christians.
8. The first Christians did not neglect meeting together.
9. The first Christians fostered friendships with each other.

Personal Story:
Steps of Faith

There was no dramatic conversion or radical life change. Glennie's decision to become a Christian was just a small step of faith in a Godward direction.

Like her husband, Darin, Glennie was considered a good person. She grew up believing in God and wanted to go to heaven when she died. But by the time Glennie was in junior high she had stopped going to church and only prayed when she was in trouble or needed something. Like many good people, Glennie had no idea what it meant to have a relationship with Jesus—until she met Kathy.

Glennie's neighbor, Kathy, was a Christian. As the two women became friends Glennie watched Kathy live out her relationship with Jesus. It wasn't merely her involvement in church; love was evident when Kathy interacted with other people. Peace was obvious when she dealt with difficult situations.

The neighbors talked more and more about spiritual things. Glennie had a lot of questions about God and faith. Initially, she wanted the peace and love she saw in Kathy's life. Over time, Glennie began to wonder if what she needed was Jesus.

When Kathy invited Glennie to attend a women's Bible study class, she cautiously accepted. As the class talked about the Creation, Glennie realized she believed God made the world. Even though she did not understand *how* He did it, she put her faith in God as Creator. When the class talked about Jesus, Glennie took another step of faith. She believed Jesus's death on the Cross paid the penalty her sins had earned.

Then Glennie took her most important step of faith— she asked Jesus to become her Savior and Lord. "When the pastor asked me if I wanted to give my life to Jesus, my answer was yes. I remembered wondering if I was ready because my faith seemed so small. I still had lots of questions. But I believed God could do anything."

As a new Christian, Glennie's walk of faith had just begun. She learned to believe in the power of prayer. In the midst of serious health concerns with both her father and father-in-law, Glennie asked her Bible study leaders to pray with her. Peace filled Glennie as they prayed together; she knew God heard their prayers.

Glennie continued to study the Bible. As her small group read about the life of Jesus in the Book of John, Glennie was aware of the presence of God's Spirit. "I felt very blessed for the intimate gift of the Holy Spirit. I knew He was helping me understand the Bible."

Allowing God to guide her life was another step of faith. But every new experience taught Glennie that God could be trusted. "I have peace knowing God is in control of my life. If He can make the oceans and the mountains He can certainly take care of me." (Read about Glennie's husband, Darin, in session 4.)

• •

✤ FIND OUT MORE ✤

In this session, we learned about the audience's response to the very first Christian sermon. When Peter shared the good news about Jesus's death and resurrection, 3,000 people responded by putting their faith in Jesus. The first thing they did, *after* accepting the message of Jesus, was to receive baptism. Let's take a closer look at this important act of obedience.

Read Mark 1:4–11. This man named John had been sent by God to prepare the way for Jesus. He spent his time preaching to the people and calling them to be baptized. This baptism was a symbolic way to show they had repented of their sins. Repentant hearts are hearts ready to receive Jesus.

As we previously studied in session 4, Jesus was sinless. (See Hebrews 4:15.) He was not baptized to be cleansed from sin.

Q: What happened when Jesus came up out of the water? What kind of impression do you think this made on the crowd?

Read Romans 6:3–8. *(You read this passage last session.)* Baptism is a physical picture of a spiritual reality. The Greek word translated as *baptism* means "to dip." (For more on the meaning of the word *baptism*, see *Vine's Complete Expository Dictionary of Old and New Testament Words.*) It refers to a process of submersion and emergence. Mark 1:10, which you read above, tells us Jesus was in the Jordan River for His baptism.

Q: Describe the parallel between the physical act of baptism and the spiritual reality of becoming a follower of Jesus as found in Romans 6:3–8. Keep the definition of baptism in mind to help with your answer.

Jesus's baptism set the example for His followers. All through the Book of Acts we see examples of individuals being baptized after giving their lives to Jesus. The act of baptism is symbolic of the forgiveness and new life believers receive from Jesus. Christ followers have "died" to their old life of sin and been "resurrected" to a new life of obedience.

How Do I Get to Know God?

*W*hen I first met Connie, I didn't know much about her. But it didn't take long to realize I wanted her to be my friend. Connie, outgoing and fun, is always the life of the party. And if there isn't a party, she starts one.

Back then, Connie walked regularly for exercise. She had a different walking buddy for every day of the week. When "Wednesday" moved away she asked if I was interested. Walking with Connie became part of my regular routine.

Up to then, I had not spent much time with Connie. At first, our walking conversations were light and casual. We had to get to know each other. Connie was interested in my life, and she was a good listener. Slowly, I began to share more serious and important things with her. She did the same with me. We became close friends and learned to trust one another.

My time with Connie expanded beyond the Wednesday walk appointment. We had heart-to-hearts over coffee (tea for Connie) and the occasional lunch. Connie became one of those very few people in my life I can talk to about anything. I know everything I share is safe with her. We began to refer to our serious conversations as "walk talk" even if we were on the phone. These things were just between us.

When my husband's company moved our family, Connie had to find a new "Wednesday" once again. Yet, we've stayed close with email, regular phone conversations, and the occasional plane trip for a visit.

Initially, my friendship with Connie grew because we regularly spent time together. It deepened, because once trust was tested and proved, we each leaned on that trust again and again.

In this session, we will explore why Christians need to spend time with God and what it might look like. If you have recently given your life to Jesus, you are in the beginning stages of a new friendship with the God of all creation. This relationship will not become close overnight. It will take a commitment on your part to regularly spend time with Jesus. Talk to Him, share your heart. Let Him talk to you through the Bible. Learn to trust Him because He is completely trustworthy.

God's Purpose for You: To Become Like Jesus

If you have a relationship with Jesus through faith, you have been saved from the eternal death that sin brings. Instead, you will spend eternity in the presence of God. As wonderful as that is, God wants more for your life now. First, He wants you to experience the joy and peace that come through intimacy with Him. Second, God wants you to be like Jesus. The Bible tells us God knew His children in advance and He *chose them to become like his Son*" (Romans 8:29 NLT).

Q: Consider what you've learned about Jesus and His character during this study. List some ways you think God wants you to be like Jesus.

Read 2 Corinthians 3:13–18 in your Bible or in the margin.

Moses was God's chosen leader for the people of Israel. With God's power and direction he led them out of slavery in Egypt approximately 1,400 years before Jesus was born, though the exact date is unknown. Moses regularly met with God and related

His commands to the people. The Bible says God spoke to Moses *"face to face, as a man speaks with his friend"* (Exodus 33:11). After spending time in His presence, Moses's face brightly reflected God's glory. With this radiant face, Moses would relate God's words to the people. Then Moses would cover his face with a veil until he met with God again.

Moses was the only one who talked to God face to face. Moses was the only one who got close enough to reflect God's glory. In the 2 Corinthians passage Paul uses this story about Moses to illustrate the privilege and freedom Christians have in our relationship with God.

> We are not like Moses, who put a veil over his face so the people of Israel would not see the glory, even though it was destined to fade away. But the people's minds were hardened, and to this day whenever the old covenant is being read, the same veil covers their minds so they cannot understand the truth. And this veil can be removed only by believing in Christ. Yes, even today when they read Moses's writings, their hearts are covered with that veil, and they do not understand.
>
> But whenever someone turns to the Lord, the veil is taken away. For the Lord is the Spirit, and wherever the Spirit of the Lord is, there is freedom. So all of us who have had that veil removed can see and reflect the glory of the Lord. And the Lord—who is the Spirit—makes us more and more like him as we are changed into his glorious image.
>
> —2 Corinthians 3:13–18 (NLT)

Q: According to 2 Corinthians 3:14–15, what limited the Israelites' understanding of the Old Covenant? (Note: *Old Covenant* refers to God's revelation and law to His people before Jesus came. The purpose of the Old Covenant or Old Testament was to illustrate the people's need for a Savior and point the way to Jesus.)

Q: According to verses 16–18, why are Christians more fully able to understand the things of God?

In session 6, we learned sin brings spiritual death. However, when we turn to Jesus in repentance and accept the forgiveness He offers, we receive the gift of the Holy Spirit. God's Spirit gives new life—eternal life—to our once-dead spirits. This is what it means to be born again.

The person without God's Spirit cannot understand spiritual things. But the Holy Spirit's presence enables us to understand the things of God. For only the Spirit of God knows the mind of God. (See 1 Corinthians 2:10–14.) Because of Christ, Christians also have the freedom, like Moses, to enter into God's presence. While we spend time with Him, the Holy Spirit not only helps us talk to Him, He also helps us understand more about who God is.

Reread 2 Corinthians 3:17–18.

Q: How do you think spending time with God helps Christians to become more like Jesus?

To be like Jesus we have to know Him and what He's like. The only way to do that is to spend time with Him. We need to talk to Him through prayer and let Him talk to us through the Bible. As we regularly sit in God's presence our character begins to reflect the character of Jesus, like Moses's face reflected the glory of God.

Getting to Know Jesus: Spending Time with God

When you spend time with your best friend who does the talking? You or your friend? If you are like most friends, you take turns talking and listening. That's how it should be in our time with God. We talk to God. We listen while God talks to us.

Christians use the term *spiritual disciplines* to refer to specific activities that help us know God better and encourage our spiritual growth (becoming more like Jesus). Two of these activities are prayer and Bible reading. (There are others, but we will focus on these primary ones.)

What is prayer? Simply put, prayer is talking to God. You can talk out loud or silently in your heart and mind. But why is it so important?

1. It is an act of obedience. Over and over in the Bible God tells us to pray. When we obey it is the beginning of yielding our lives to the will and activity of God.

2. It is an expression and strengthening of our faith. When we pray it reveals we expect God to hear and answer. Then when He proves Himself faithful to hear and answer, that experience strengthens our faith and deepens our trust in Him.

3. It is our soul's cry to God. Even though prayer takes discipline, it is more than just routinely talking to God. God invites us to bring Him our needs, our problems, our hurts, and our longings through prayer.

The Bible gives us glimpses into Jesus's prayer life. I've heard people joke by asking, "Since Jesus is God, when He prayed wasn't He just talking to Himself?" We can't fully understand the triune nature of God, but Scripture does teach that God is three distinct persons. So, even though I don't fully understand it, God the Son did talk to God the Father in prayer. If Jesus needed to pray, how much more must we?

Q: Read the following Scriptures and describe what each one reveals about Jesus's prayer life.

- Matthew 14:22–23 (Note: This was immediately after Jesus performed a tremendous miracle.)

- Mark 1:35

- Luke 5:15–16

- Luke 6:12–13

Many Christians pray while they're driving, exercising, or working in the garden. They "pray as they go." These times of prayer perfectly illustrate the Bible's command to *"pray continually"* (1 Thessalonians 5:17). However, if a Christian *only* prays on the go he is not following the example Jesus set.

Time alone in prayer was Jesus's regular habit. He needed it to carry out His ministry in obedience to the Father. He prayed before major decisions. He prayed after huge success. Prayer was His lifeline to God. Every Christian must have regular time in focused prayer. We cannot fully concentrate on God when our attention is divided.

Q: Draw lines to match the following verses to the corresponding characteristics of prayer that please God.

Romans 12:12	Be devoted to prayer, watchful, and faithful.
Ephesians 6:18	Pray faithfully.
Philippians 4:6	With the Spirit's guidance, be alert; don't stop.
Colossians 4:2	Pray about everything.

Q: Considering the characteristics above, describe what your prayer life should look like.

You may be wondering what you should pray about. "Everything" is the Bible's general answer. However, Scripture also teaches about many specific types of prayer. We don't have time to talk about all of them here, but I will mention several we should engage in regularly.

- Repentance—Confessing specific sins and asking for God's forgiveness
- Worship—Acknowledging the divine attributes of God and praising Him for them
- Thanksgiving—Thanking God for what He has done

- Petition—Asking God for help for yourself, someone else, or a situation

To get the feel for the different kinds of prayer, write a brief prayer to God below in each category we mentioned.

- Repentance

- Worship

- Thanksgiving

- Petition

In session 1 we explored how God reveals Himself through the Bible. Bible reading should accompany our focused time in prayer. When we read it during our quiet time with God, He uses His Word to speak to us and shape our lives.

How do you know where to start? Cracking open the Bible and picking a verse with your finger isn't a good way. You don't want to be random in reading God's Word. It's best to have a system to keep you moving purposefully through the Bible. One way to get started is to pick a book of the Bible that interests you and read a small section a day until you finish the book. The Books of Mark or John are great places to start. Also, at the back of this book, you can find a sample Bible reading plan and some Scripture memory guides. Use one of them or find another plan that suits you.

How to Have a Quiet Time

Many Christians have questions about what to do during their focused times with God, or quiet times. Here are some suggestions.

1.   Establish a regular place and time. We are creatures of habit. If we know when and where we will meet with God daily, we are much more likely to do it. Build it into your daily schedule. If this is new for you, start small. Commit to 15–20 minutes a day and God will grow it. Keep all your "tools" (such as a Bible, journal, and pen) together in your designated spot so you'll always be prepared.

2.   Start with prayer. Ask God to speak to you and help you understand His Word today. Thank Him for meeting with you.

3.   Begin to read the Bible. Remember your purpose is to communicate with God. Expect God to speak to you through His Word. Don't read hastily just to get through the passage. Let God stop you as you read to emphasize a point.

4.   Meditate on the passage. Meditation is not emptying your mind. It is deep thinking on spiritual truths. As you read, linger over verses that impact you. Ask God questions and "listen" for His answers. Does this passage reveal something you should: believe about God? praise or thank or trust God for?   pray about for yourself or others? make a decision about? act on?

5.   Pray as you read. Time with God should be interactive. Respond to God as He speaks to you through His Word.

6.   Journal. Record what God says to you and how you will respond. Writing can help you stay focused on God and His voice.

7.   Memorize. Commit to memorize verses that you feel will be especially helpful to you. Knowing Scripture by heart helps us guard against sin, reminds us of God's promises, provides guidance, and allows us to meditate on God's Word anywhere and anytime. (You will find "Scripture Memory Tips" and some memorization plans in the back of this book.)

8.   Application. Apply to your life whatever God says to you through prayer and His Word. It may be repentance. It may be a change in behavior. It may be a specific action. But whatever it is, do it.

Session Summary

If you are a Christian, God wants you to become more and more like Jesus. God will shape and mold your character as you spend time with Him in prayer and Bible reading. It is an amazing privilege and blessing to be in the presence of the God of the universe. Commit now to spending time with Him regularly.

• •

Personal Story:
Strength in the Hard Times

It happened Sunday, May 24, 2002, just before lunch. That's the exact time Laura gave her life to Jesus. She remembers it well because the moment divides her life in half—the part she lived without God and the part she now lives with Him.

When Laura became a Christian, her mother was fighting breast cancer. Within three years Laura's mother and father had died, and her husband had left her.

Laura can't imagine living through those years without her faith in Jesus. "God literally held me up. His big arms wrapped around me when I needed Him."

Growing up, Laura rarely attended church. She thought about God and spiritual things but not enough to really seek Him. When Laura's three sons were little she wanted them to be in church. She took them for awhile, but it didn't last.

When Laura's oldest son, Kurt, was in high school, he began attending church and a Bible study group with a friend. Laura felt angry. She believed she should take her kids to church, not someone else. This reaction prodded her to try church again. Things happened quickly after that. She visited the church Kurt was attending and within a couple of weeks she found herself in a Bible study. "One minute I was mad and the next I was sitting in a Bible study class," Laura remembers.

God chose this time to reveal Himself to Laura. She learned something new and amazing about God each week. "Studying the Bible showed me why I needed God. All my insides were wrong. I didn't hold back once I knew I needed Him."

Although Laura's husband, Brad, did not want anything to do with Jesus, he did not try to stop her from pursuing her new faith or from taking her two younger sons to church.

Even though Brad allowed Laura and the boys to attend church, he became the source of a lot of heartache. He not only walked away from their marriage, but also from a large debt that landed squarely on Laura. She was forced to sell their home. Many days she even wondered how she would feed her children.

Yet in every instance God provided. Laura began to pray and depend on Him. God taught her more and more about Himself. Laura learned He answers prayers. Laura also learned that the answer isn't always what she wants, but it is always what she needs.

God is helping Laura through the most difficult time of her life. She feels close to Him. He is strengthening and growing her as a mom and as a person. Each day is filled with His provision and blessings. Doing life without God isn't an option.

• • • • • • • • • • • • • • • • • • • •

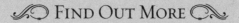

FIND OUT MORE

Scripture is full of amazing promises about the power of prayer. There are numerous examples in the Bible of prayer's miraculous effect. From physical healing to deliverance, from danger to restoration of life, God's power is extended to His people through prayer.

Read the following Scripture passages and record the powerful possibilities of prayer.

James 1:5

1 John 1:9

Philippians 4:6–7

James 5:13–16

John 15:7

1 John 5:13–15

A few of these passages include conditions for effective prayer. Look back through the verses and list any of these conditions you find.

....
....
....
....
....
....
....

How Do I Follow God?

*W*ayne and I have "misplaced" our children several times over the years. Mark was only a toddler when we lost him at an air show. Sarah has been separated from us twice—once at Disney World and once at a ski resort in the Canadian Rockies. A lot of her family stories start like this: "Let me tell you about the time my parents left me at..."

Have you ever been lost in a crowd? Many times in order to keep from being separated from my companions in a throng I've had to either hold on to them or follow right on their heels, not taking my eyes off them. If I hadn't followed their every move I would have been lost and on my own.

Following God's leading takes similar diligence. He has given us everything we need to live a life that pleases and honors Him. We have His revealed Word in the Bible. And if you are a Christian, you have God's Spirit within you to teach, counsel, and guide you at every step. But it is our responsibility to listen and obey.

Following God's Lead: Life in the Spirit

Every time we turn on a television or surf the Internet, we are bombarded with messages encouraging us to do our own thing and make our own decisions. After all, we are our own boss, no one can tell us what to do. But that mind-set runs contrary to God's truth. Remember, if you are a Christian, your life is no longer your own. You belong to God.

Read 1 Corinthians 6:19–20.

Q: According to this passage, why do Christians belong to God?

Q: How should this truth affect the way you live?

Q: According to verse 19, what unique connection do Christians have with God?

God is present in the lives of His children by His Spirit dwelling in us. What an amazing thought! God does not ask us to follow and obey Him and then just leave us to make it on our own. He is with us every moment.

Read Romans 8:5–12. In this passage are several important truths about a Christian's relationship with the Holy Spirit. The following summary statements are found in this passage. If necessary, reread the verses to help you fill in the blanks of the following statements.

Q: The Christian who follows his own natural desires cannot
_____ God.

Q: But the Christian who is controlled by the Spirit will experience
_____ and _____. If you belong to Christ, the
_____ of _____ lives in you. Christians have
an _____ to live according to the Spirit and not
follow our own natural desires.

God wants you to have an abundant life filled with His joy and
peace. This is not possible if we stubbornly follow our own ways
and desires. However, as you follow the Holy Spirit's guidance
you begin to fulfill God's purpose for your life. A life of obedience
not only pleases God, it fosters intimacy with Him. Nothing else
can offer you the same joy and peace as an intimate relationship
with your Creator.

How do we know what God wants us to do? How do we follow the guidance of the Holy Spirit? The primary way we know
God's will for us is through the Bible. As we hear it taught and as
we read and study it for ourselves we learn about God's character
and broad principles for living. Additionally, as we spend time in
prayer, the Spirit of God within us helps us understand and apply
God's Word to our lives in specific ways.

Read 1 Corinthians 2:11–14.

Q: How is the Holy Spirit able to help Christians know God's
will for them?

Q: Why are Christians able to understand spiritual things that
non-Christians can't?

It will take time to recognize God's "voice" and become sensitive to the leading of the Holy Spirit. However, as you are obedient to what you "hear," and you become more experienced in following God, recognizing the Spirit's leading will become more natural. As you live a life in the Spirit, God will continually transform your character to His.

Q: Read Galatians 5:16–25. Fill in the table below based on the content of the passage.

Characteristics of a life that follows its sinful nature	Characteristics of a life that follows the Holy Spirit

Which side of the table does your life look most like right now? No matter what your life looks like now, God wants to shape it to be more like Jesus. Write a prayer to God asking Him to help you follow His leading every day.

Failing to Follow: Getting Back on Track

God calls us to obedience, but none of us will ever be perfect this side of heaven. Our desire should be to follow God more closely today than we did yesterday. Some days we will stay close to Him and obediently follow His leading. And sadly, some days we will choose to ignore God and do things our own way. What should we do when we've chosen to disobey God? Whether it's one small thing or a string of disobedience over a long period of time, our response should be the same.

Read James 4:1–10. James, the inspired author, is writing to Christians who are not following God closely. The first six verses of this passage describe the effects of their giving into their fleshly desires.

Q: Look again at verses 7–10. List the verbs found in this passage that describe the actions a Christian should take when they've chosen his or her own way over God's. (I spotted ten!)

People still sin after becoming Christians. Although we belong to God and have His Spirit within us to teach, guide, and empower us, we still choose our own sinful way sometimes. But there's good news.

Q: Read 1 John 1:9 and write God's promise below.

This verse reinforces what we read in James 4. When Christians sin, God calls us to humble ourselves before Him in repentance. When we turn from sin and draw near to Him, He promises to forgive us (1 John 1:9) and lift us up (James 4:10).

A Final Word to Study Participants

If you have become a Christian during this study, I praise God for your new life in Him. God has put His Spirit within you to transform you on a daily basis into the likeness of His Son. And when you sin you can come to Him in repentance and receive forgiveness, as we've learned in this session. Get to know your Savior intimately through regular prayer and Bible study. Become an active member of a Bible-based church. Remember God saved you into His body.

I must leave new believers with a word of caution. Just as a couple enjoys a honeymoon phase in their new marriage, new believers may experience a similar time in their new relationship with Christ. After a time, however, just as most newlyweds discover that marriage takes work to make it work, new believers will discover that living the Christian life takes effort. Old sin habits may be hard to break; finding time to spend with God may be difficult. But remember, God has given you His Holy Spirit to help you become obedient to Him. Rely on God and continue to *"work out your salvation,"* while depending on Him. (See Philippians 2:12–13.)

If you have not made a decision to trust Jesus as your Savior and Lord, turning your life over to Him, then why haven't you? You were created by and for Him. Your life can never be what God intended until you surrender it to Him. Your present life and eternal destiny depend on it. Why not make that decision now?

• • • • • • • • • • • • • • • • • • • •

Personal Story:
Following God Through Ups and Downs

God had never been a part of their marriage. They had never taken their daughters to church. But all that changed one summer.

Jeff and Brenda had both spent a little time in church growing up. They were married in the church in Brenda's hometown. But when they started married life together, Sundays became a good day to sleep in. Spiritual things dropped to the bottom of their priority list.

Then one summer, years later, Brenda took their two girls to Vacation Bible School at a local church. It seemed like a good thing to do. When the week was over the girls insisted they go to church as a family.

What began as religious routine for Jeff and Brenda soon changed their lives. The church offered a beginning Bible study class, which Jeff and Brenda attended. It was a pivotal time for both of them.

"Jeff and I had never studied the Bible before. What we learned about God was overwhelming," Brenda relates.

Jeff's experience was similar. "Participating in the Bible study was the turning point. I had always thought I was going to hell when I died because of the rough times in my life, but I learned that God loves me unconditionally. He offers forgiveness to those who repent of their sin and put their faith in Him."

During the course of the Bible study, the couple was facing difficulties with the small business Jeff was operating. It was struggling financially and Brenda's job could barely support the family. The stress affected the girls emotionally and academically. Finally, Jeff and Brenda decided they had no choice but to close the business, move back to their hometown, and start over. But God had other plans.

They ran into a couple from church one night at the grocery store and talked to them about their decision. The couple encouraged Jeff and Brenda to pray and ask God to show them what they should do. By the next day it was obvious God wanted them to stay. Through prayer and new circumstances, He gave Jeff and Brenda clear direction.

Eventually the business did close, but God continued to guide them. Looking back, Jeff knows even that was part of God's plan. "God used the failing of our business to get my attention. It was a step in my faith journey."

Brenda agrees. "During that trial God reached out to us through the people of the church. They showed us how to trust in God and His plan for our lives. Jeff and I realized we didn't want to do life without God anymore."

That's when Jeff and Brenda decided to give their lives to Jesus. They told the church about their decision and were baptized together.

Today they can't imagine trying to live life without following Jesus. Jeff explains: "When we became Christians a huge burden was lifted off our lives. Now we have purpose. Now Jesus is in control. He gives us clear direction."

God has also faithfully provided for their family. Jeff now has a career he loves with a Christian radio station. He and Brenda have been able to help others, both spiritually and financially, even as God has helped them. In addition to their active involvement with their church and community, Jeff and Brenda are giving their time and money to help an orphanage in Haiti.

Jeff says they want to keep their relationship with God close and follow His plan for them. "We hope God will use our family to positively impact others for Him. So we just try to faithfully follow His direction every day."

• •

On the night He was betrayed, Jesus shared many important "last things" with His disciples. He reinforced that He was the only way to the Father. He told them to expect the Holy Spirit. And He gave them a beautiful word picture to illustrate the life of discipleship. Jesus and His disciples may have even walked passed a vineyard that night as He used the familiar grape vine to describe the close relationship that Jesus's followers should have with Him.

Read John 15:5–17 and answer the following questions.

Q: In your relationship with Jesus, who is the "vine?" Who is the "branch?"

Q: The Greek word translated as "remain" can also be translated as "abide," "dwell," and "continue." With this in mind, describe what it looks like for a Christian to "remain" in Jesus.

Q: What will be the results when a Christian—a disciple of Jesus—remains in Him? (Be sure and look through the entire passage.)

To live the life of discipleship Jesus describes, we must be constantly and consistently connected to Him. Like the branch needs the vine for its very life, a Christian should cling to Christ in total dependence and trust. When we do, our lives will affect eternity and bring God glory!

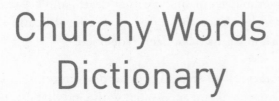

Churchy Words Dictionary

Born again—to be born anew or from above
Usage: to be spiritually reborn by the Spirit of God; term synonymous with "Christian"

Faith—having a solid confidence, trust, hope, and active reliance in God and His promises
Usage: results in personal commitment and obedience to God

Inspiration—God's supernatural direction to a messenger to accurately record what God wants to communicate to humankind; works through the messenger's own personality, intelligence, and style while not compromising God's message
Usage: The Bible is the inspired Word of God, God's message to us physically written by human agents.

Justification—making one righteous (see *righteous* below) who is not righteous or just
Usage: the guilty verdict, earned by an individual's sin, is erased because Jesus paid the penalty; individuals who trust in Jesus are declared not guilty

Lost—refers to the condition of spiritual death caused by sin
Usage: describes an individual whose relationship with God is broken because of his or her sin; eternal separation from God because of sin

Redemption—deliverance by payment of a price
Usage: term used in slave trade (prior to salvation we were slaves to sin); deliverance from sin, spiritual death, and separation from God provided by Jesus through His sacrificial death; those who put their faith in Jesus have been redeemed

Repent/Repentance—to change or alter one's mind
Usage: recognition of sin; agreement with God that one is a sinner; a "turning away" from sin and a "turning to" God

Resurrection—literally, "to stand again"
Usage: a rising of a body from the grave; Jesus's physical return to life after His death; also refers to an event at the end of history when Jesus will return to earth and those who've already died and belong to Him will join Him and receive new bodies

Revelation—literal translation means an "unveiling"
Usage: describes what God makes known to mankind about Himself and His ways; accomplished first through Scripture (the Bible) and ultimately through Jesus Christ; God's purpose in revelation is for us to know Him

Righteous/Righteousness—conformity to God's perfect moral standard
Usage: impossible for us to accomplish on our own; Jesus gives His righteousness to those who trust in Him for salvation

Salvation—delivery from sin and its consequences
Usage: eternal life now and forevermore in the presence of God

Saved—having been born again; received salvation
Usage: see *born again*

Sin—to "miss the mark" as in an arrow missing a bull's-eye; to deviate from the norm

Usage: not adhering to the pattern God established for mankind; choosing our own way over God's way; also used as a noun to refer to our wrong thinking, actions, and corrupted nature

Bible Reading Plan
for New Christians:
31 Days to Know
God's Plan for Us

This plan is a general overview of God's dealings with humanity; our responses to Him; and how He gives us hope, salvation, and an eternal future.

DAY	THEME	PASSAGE
1	The fall of humanity	Genesis 3:1–19
2	A people set for God	Genesis 12:1–3; 28:10–15; 32:22–28
3	The Ten Commandments	Exodus 20:1–17
4	Sacrifices and the Law	Leviticus 5:14–19
5	Dealing with sin under the Law	Leviticus 20:7–27
6	Obedience from love	Deuteronomy 6:1–9; 11:13–21
7	Humanity's disobedience	Judges 2:10–19
8	The people demand a king	1 Samuel 8
9	Saul fails and is rejected	1 Samuel 15:17–23
10	God's people break His covenant	Jeremiah 11:1–17

11	The people's history of rebellion	Ezekiel 20:5–26
12	An eternal king promised	Jeremiah 23:1–6; Isaiah 9:6–7; Zechariah 9:9–10
13	The promised Christ is born	Luke 2:1–20
14	The Word became flesh	John 1:1–18
15	Signs and wonders of Jesus	Matthew 9:1–8; Luke 13:10–17
16	Jesus fulfills the Law	Matthew 5:17–20; Romans 8:1–4
17	Jesus teaches about new life	John 3
18	Jesus's arrest	John 18:1–11
19	Jesus's death and resurrection	Luke 23:44 to 24:12
20	Christ is sacrifice for all	Hebrews 10:1–18; 11:1–3; 12:1–3
21	God's righteous wrath explained	Romans 1:18–32
22	God's judgment explained	Romans 2:5–11
23	Saved by grace alone	Ephesians 2
24	Righteousness by faith	Romans 3:9–26
25	Life through Christ	Romans 5:12–21
26	Life by the Spirit	Romans 8:1–17; Galatians 5:16–26
27	Living sacrifices	Romans 12
28	Walking in the light	1 John 1–2
29	Living for God	1 Peter 4:1–11
30	Love for one another	1 John 3:11–24
31	Promise of eternity	2 Corinthians 5:1–10; Revelation 21:1–4

Reprinted with permission.

Plan developed by Dr. Richard J. Krejcir.

© *Into Thy Word 1983, inspired from an old Episcopal competitive devotion, originally developed for Campus Crusade for Christ (www.intothyword.org).*

Scripture Memory Tips

Always be prepared to give an answer to everyone who asks you to give the reason for the hope that you have.
—1 Peter 3:15

Memorizing God's Word successfully takes commitment, persistence, and work. However, it is a discipline that will reap many rewards in a Christian's life. When you hide the truth of God's Word in your heart it is then available for His use. God will use it to guide you, comfort you, and transform you to be more like Jesus. Additionally, you will always be ready to give an answer to everyone for the hope you have in Christ.

1. Have a plan.

- Decide on a timetable for memorization. Will you memorize one verse a week or one a month. Don't overwhelm yourself. Start simple and plan for success. If you are fairly new to Scripture memory, start with shorter, uncomplicated verses.

- Use a list of Scriptures someone else has compiled.

- Make your own list based on what God is doing in your life right now. For example: Is God calling you to witness? To live a holy life? To foster humility? Make a list of applicable verses. You can find resources online or perhaps listed in the back of your Bible to help you.

- Memorize sections of Scripture one verse at a time.

2. Write out the verses.
- Use sheets of paper or index cards to write out each verse to memorize. Use one sheet per verse.

3. Have a storage system.
- Use a binder or an index card box to file and store your verses for review.

4. Know the context.
- Before you start to memorize, read the entire section of Scripture surrounding your chosen verse. Know the setting and occasion for this verse of Scripture. By reading the section in which the verse appears, you'll get a fuller understanding of the verse's meaning and significance. If you do this, you are less likely to misapply or misuse the verse in your daily life.

5. Use various methods to memorize.
- Write the verse. Write down the verse and the reference every day during the initial memorization process.

- Verbalize the verse. Say the verse silently to yourself and out loud. Start phrase by phrase, working up to the entire verse with the reference.

- Hear the verse. Record the verse in some way and play it back.

- See the verse. Use additional index cards or sticky notes to put your verse in prominent places where you will encounter it during the day. For example: bathroom mirror, refrigerator door, laundry room wall.

- Create visual reminders. Draw pictures that symbolize your verse. For instance, for Psalm 119:11 you could draw a Bible inside a heart to depict the idea of hiding God's Word in your heart.

6. Be "Word perfect."
- Memorize the verse word for word, along with the reference. Set a high standard for yourself as you learn the verses and don't consider them memorized until you have every word correct.

7. Review, review, review.
- The one week or one month you spend memorizing a verse will never be sufficient to retain it forever. You must have a system for review. Set a number of verses to review each week. Review new verses every week for a time and then review them less and less frequently. Use "dead time" to review verses. For example: when you're stuck in traffic, waiting in lines, holding on the phone.

Scripture Memory Plan:
The Basics

*I*f this is your first time to memorize Scripture, you may want to pick one of the two passages listed below to memorize each month. If you are ready for more of a challenge, memorize both passages each month.

Note: The Scriptures for January through May will prepare and equip you to tell other people about your faith.

Month	Topic	Passage
January	Jesus the only Way	John 14:6 Acts 4:12
February	Our need for a Savior	Romans 3:23 Romans 6:23
March	Christ our sinless, perfect sacrifice	2 Corinthians 5:21 Hebrews 4:15
April	Christ's payment through death for our sins	Romans 5:8 1 Peter 3:18
May	Salvation by grace through faith	Ephesians 2:8–9 Romans 10:9–10

June	Living for Christ	Galatians 2:20 Romans 6:10–11
July	The importance of God's Word	Hebrews 4:12 2 Timothy 3:16–17
August	Our response to trials	James 1:2–4 1 Peter 1:6–7
September	Living fruitful lives	Galatians 5:22–23 John 15:5
October	Conforming our minds to God's will	1 Peter 1:13 Romans 12:1–2
November	The Holy Spirit in us	Romans 8:9 1 Corinthians 6:19–20
December	Living a life of discipleship	Luke 9:23 John 13:35

Scripture Memory Plan:
A Section a Month

Month	Subject	Passage
January	Perfection of God's Word	Psalm 19:1–14
February	Repentance and Forgiveness	Psalm 32:1–11
March	Praise to God	1 Chronicles 16:23–24
April	Sovereignty of God	Isaiah 40:21–31
May	Prophecy of Christ	Isaiah 53:1–12
June	The Incarnation	John 1:1–14
July	Jesus Our Example	Philippians 2:5–11
August	Abiding in Christ	John 15:1–17
September	Dead to Sin/Alive to Christ	Romans 6:1–14
October	Life in the Spirit	Romans 8:15–17
November	Love in the Church	1 Corinthians 13:1–13
December	Armor of God	Ephesians 6:10–18

Recommended Resources

Recommended books to help you grow in your faith and knowledge:

Basic Christianity by John Stott
This classic presents and defends the Christian faith and shows how it should be lived out in the life of every believer.

Can Man Live Without God? by Ravi Zacharias
Zacharias defends the existence of God and the validity of the Christian faith, emphasizing the impact of God's existence on every area of life.

The Case for Faith by Lee Strobel
A former atheist, Strobel overcomes eight persistent objections to belief, thus removing intellectual barriers to the Christian faith. See also his *The Case for a Creator, The Case for Christ,* and *The Case for Easter.*

Essential Truths of the Christian Faith by R. C. Sproul
Renowned theologian Sproul explains more than 100 major Christian doctrines in a way every reader can understand.

Fueled by Faith by Jennifer Kennedy Dean
Dean helps readers examine the role of faith in their prayer lives. Also: *Live a Praying Life* is Dean's foundational work on prayer.

Growing Your Faith: How to Mature in Christ by Jerry Bridges
Bridges helps readers learn how to deepen their relationship with Jesus through spending time in the Bible, relying on the Holy Spirit, and serving others.

Jesus Among Other Gods by Ravi Zacharias
Are all religions equally true? Zacharias compares Jesus with the founders of other world religions, revealing Jesus' supremacy.

Know Why You Believe by Paul E. Little
Little tackles the tough questions about Christianity and provides solid answers to build your faith.

Now That's a Good Question by R. C. Sproul
Sproul answers frequently asked questions about Christianity.

Prayer 101: What Every Intercessor Needs to Know by Elaine Helms
This practical guidebook helps readers learn how to express their relationship with God through prayer.

Web sites to strengthen and encourage your faith:

www.answersingenesis.org
www.bethinking.org
www.christianbook.com
www.christianitytoday.com
www.crosswalk.com
www.kathyhoward.org
www.reasons.org
www.wayofthemaster.org
www.wmu.com

Sources referenced in this book:

Baker, Warren. *The Complete Word Study Old Testament*. Chattanooga: AMG Publishers, 1994.

Fernando, Ajith. *The NIV Application Commentary: Acts*. Grand Rapids: Zondervan, 1998.

Grudem, Wayne. *Systematic Theology: An Introduction to Biblical Doctrine*. Leicester, England and Grand Rapids: Inter-Varsity Press and Zondervan, a joint publication, 1994.

"The Jewish historian Flavius Josephus." http://www.facing thechallenge.org/josephus.php (accessed October 14, 2009)

Lockyer, Herbert. *All the Apostles of the Bible*. Grand Rapids: Zondervan, 1972.

McDowell, Josh. *Evidence That Demands a Verdict: Historical Evidences for the Christian Faith*, rev. ed. San Bernardino: Here's Life Publishers, 1979.

"Ranks of Scientists Doubting Darwin's Theory on the Rise." http://www.discovery.org/scripts/viewDB/index .php?command=view&id=2732 (accessed September 21, 2009)

Story, Dan. *Defending Your Faith: Reliable Answers for a New Generation of Seekers and Skeptics*. Grand Rapids: Kregel Publications, 1997.

Whiston, William, trans. *The Works of Josephus, Complete and Unabridged, New Updated Edition*. Peabody, MA: Hendrickson Publishers, 1987.

Zodhiates, Spiros. *The Complete Word Study New Testament*. Chattanooga: AMG Publishers, 1991.

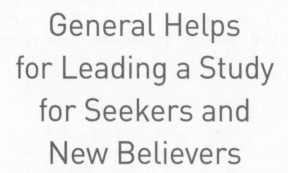

General Helps
for Leading a Study
for Seekers and
New Believers

*L*eading spiritual seekers and new Christians in a study of God's Word is an exciting and rewarding experience. You will witness God's activity in their lives from a front-row seat. Plus, studying again the foundational truths of your faith will enrich your own life.

Your approach to guiding people with little, if any, Bible knowledge in a study of Scripture will differ significantly from your approach to teaching those who are mature Christians. Before you begin this adventure, take some time to review the leader helps below.

Form a group.
Consider the relationships you have right now with neighbors, co-workers, and friends. Ask your church family and other Christian friends if they know someone who has never explored the Bible before. Have any of them shown an interest in spiritual things?

Prepare a postcard or flyer to make it easy to share the important details. Make it clear this is a casual study of the basics of Christianity. Be sure to include all the details of date, place, time, and contact information.

Include verbiage on the promotional piece that will pique interest in the study. For example: *Have you ever wondered what the Bible is about? Or What is your purpose in life? Do you want to know more about God?*

Personal invitations always get the best results. Phone calls or face-to-face invites are a great way to follow up on the postcard invitation.

Be confident as you approach people, knowing that new Christians will benefit from the study by learning the foundational truths of their faith. In fact, Christians of any maturity level will be blessed by the study as they are better equipped to share their faith with others and renew their sense of gratitude to God for their salvation.

Enlist some help.

Depending on the size of your group, you will want to have one or more mature Christians participate with you. This will require careful selection and a bit of training. In addition to providing prayer support, they can also help you establish relationships with participants outside of class, keep the discussion going, and share about their relationship with God.

Be careful that your helpers don't talk too much. There is a fine line between good and timely input and monopolizing the discussion. The right amount—from them and you—will encourage the members to participate, but too much will discourage them.

There needs to be one clear group leader. Any Christian members of the group should be able to gently help the participants and not appear to be a leader. Otherwise, an us-against-them atmosphere might develop.

Pick the meeting place.

Should you meet at your church or in a home? A home is non-threatening, and individuals who don't attend church may be more likely to come. A church setting may be initially uncomfortable for some. However, once they are at ease with this new atmosphere, attending regular church services and another Bible study will be the next step. Assess your individual situation. If you have a home available in a central location with few distractions, then you may want to start there. If child care is an issue or Sundays seem to be the best time of the week for everyone, then a church classroom can work.

If possible, have your group meet around a table. This setup increases the comfort level. Food and beverages give people something to do with their hands—and mouths! Again, this is about making your group as comfortable as possible. It doesn't have to be elaborate. A pot of coffee and store-bought muffins work great.

Create a safe environment.

Assume your participants have no knowledge of the Bible. Explain to them that they are a varied group with different backgrounds. Since not everyone has the same level of knowledge about the Bible you will be starting at ground zero. This will help put people at ease. The group may include some nominal Christians, people from nonevangelical backgrounds who only have a small amount of Bible knowledge, longtime Christians, and people who know nothing at all about Christianity. As the leader you have to speak to the lowest level of knowledge.

Assure them that all questions are welcome. There is nothing too basic or silly. Give them the freedom to disagree. Don't expect them to accept everything presented in the material. This is a time of exploration. Your job is to present the truth and introduce them to Jesus. Let God take care of the rest.

Don't expect them to act or talk like your church friends. They are not familiar with church "culture" and its rules on dress or speech. What you may find offensive or unacceptable for a Christian is not only acceptable in their world, but the norm.

Guide the discussion.

Be careful with Christian jargon. Christians regularly use many words and phrases that confuse the spiritual seeker. Some should be avoided altogether. However, some are rich in spiritual truth. Clearly define these words and phrases for your group. Then, as you begin to use them during the study, reinforce their meaning so they will become a part of your group's vocabulary. *Born again* is one example of a phrase that should be defined. Not only is it rich in spiritual truth, it also comes right out of Scripture. *Asking Jesus into your heart* is a phrase you should probably avoid altogether, since it can be confusing and is not found in Scripture.

Always give guidance and plenty of time for participants to find Scripture references. For instance, if the passage is in Luke, tell them it is the third book in the New Testament. If it is in the Psalms, tell them it is roughly in the middle of their Bible.

Consider acquiring inexpensive paperback Bibles for your group. Some of your members may not own a Bible. Also, when looking up Scripture as a group, you can give a page number in addition to the reference. It is best if everyone has the same translation and page numbering.

- Review truths from previous lessons each time you meet. Don't assume they remember or that all the pieces are falling into place.

- Don't call on a specific person to read a Scripture passage, particularly the first few sessions. Read the passage yourself for at least the first two or three weeks. After that, as you sense the comfort level increasing, you can ask for a volunteer.

- Toss questions out to the group, but again, don't call on a specific person.

- Don't lecture. Keep the group time as interactive and discussion driven as possible. Of course there will be segments of time in each class when you will need to present information and biblical principles, but do this in small chunks.

- Be real, honest, and open. Don't act like you have all the answers or have it all together. This will only make them feel the Christian life is unattainable and unrealistic. Share your doubts, struggles, and failures so they can relate.

Lead in prayer.

Many of your group members will be unfamiliar and perhaps uncomfortable with prayer—especially in a group setting. Be aware of those feelings. Start slowly. You as leader should open and close in prayer for the first couple of group sessions. Don't ask anyone else to pray or take prayer requests. Don't even ask one of your Christian members to pray. Others may get nervous you will call on them next.

When you feel the group is comfortable (possibly the third session), tell them you would like to pray for their needs and concerns. Ask if anyone would like to voice a specific request before you pray. One of your Christian participants could set the example by speaking up first.

When and if you feel the group is ready, ask for a volunteer to pray. If no one speaks up quickly, then you go ahead and pray. Try it again the next week. Your goal is for your members to become comfortable with prayer.

Build relationships in and outside of class.

One-on-one time with individual members allows for more freedom to discuss deeper questions. Find common ground. Many of your participants may view Christians as "aliens." Show them you are a normal person. You aren't just a "Christian." You are a banker, a soccer mom, a friend. You go to the movies, put gas in your car, and eat pizza.

As you start this journey, begin with prayer and don't stop. Pray for yourself and each person by name. Pray that God will give you wisdom and discernment to share His Word. Pray that God will soften each person's heart to receive it.

Leader's Guide

This type of class is unique. If you have not read the "General Helps" section in this book, please do that now. If you don't plan to have a separate introductory session, use the following suggestions to kick off session 1.

Introductory Session

1. Introductions—Introduce yourself to the group and include a few personal details to provide some common ground. Ask the group members to introduce themselves. Keep it light. Don't ask them to answers questions such as "Why are you here?" or "What is your church background?"

2. Tell the group that for the purposes of this study you are assuming a ground-zero level of knowledge. (Refer to "Create a safe environment," p. 169, in the "General Helps" section for an explanation.)

3. Material—Hand out the books. If you are combining the introductory session and Session 1, it is preferable to hand out the books in advance and ask the participants to complete session 1 in preparation for the discussion. Review the way the material is organized. See this book's introduction for more information.

4. Homework—Encourage your group members to do the homework. Although not required, your members will get more out of the study if they do the lesson before your group session.

5. Self-study suggestions—Point out the "Find Out More" sections. While optional, they are designed to reinforce the truths of each session. Encourage your group members to complete them within a day or two after you meet. (Note: If participants do everything suggested, they will be completing two sections at home every week—the "Find Out More" section and the next session's material to prepare for your next group time.)

6. Foundational concepts—Review the three points on page 16. Assure the group that they do not have to agree or accept them without question but this is your starting point.

7. Tutorial on locating Bible verses—Some members of your group may have never used a Bible before. Use "Navigating Your Way Through the Bible" inset on page 20 to explain how the Bible is put together and to demonstrate how to find a specific passage.

8. If you plan an extra week for an introductory session, complete only numbers one through three of session 1 and then end your time in prayer. If you are combining your introduction with session 1, do all you want from session 1 below.

Each section below offers numerous suggestions for leading a session. You may not have time for all of them. You should not feel you have to complete them like a checklist. Select the ones you feel will best meet the needs of your particular group.

Session 1: Where Do I Begin?

1. Before the group session—If you are in a classroom with a board, write the word *faith* on it.

2. Discuss the questions about faith on page 16.

3. Ask someone to give an example of how he or she has demonstrated faith in someone or something recently. For example: Getting on an airplane and flying from one place to another demonstrates active faith in the plane and the pilot.

4. Read Hebrews 11:6 and discuss what it means to have faith in God. Discuss optional verses Ecclesiastes 3:11 or Romans 1:18–21. (Note: A full discussion of the existence of God is outside the scope of this material. If any of your group members want to explore this topic further refer them to *The Case for Faith* by Lee Strobel. You may also want to arrange to meet them privately to discuss the topic in more depth.)

5. Discuss the credibility and relevancy of the Bible.
   - Say: God has revealed Himself to us because He wants us to know Him. The Bible is one of the primary ways He does this.
   - Ask: What are some of the ways people view the Bible today?
   - Point out and discuss the section "God Makes Himself Known" on page 17.

6. Explore what the Bible says about itself and its relevance to us today.
   - Read 2 Timothy 3:16–17.
   - Look at the meaning and significance of *theopneustos* on page 19.
   - Ask: According to this passage, what are some of the uses of Scripture?
   - Read Hebrews 4:12.
   - Ask: What does this description of the Bible imply? If this is true, what attitude should we have toward the Bible?

7. Present Jesus as God's ultimate revelation.
   - Say: The Bible teaches that God's ultimate revelation is through Jesus. Christianity is unique among all the religions of the world because of the bold claims Jesus made about Himself.

- Read John 14:5–10. Give the context and background of the passage and summarize the content.
- Discuss the significance of Jesus' statement in verse 6.
- Ask: If there is a chance that Jesus truly is the only way to God, isn't His claim worth investigating?

8. Conclusion—(Consider ending every session with the following.)
- Ask if there are any other comments or questions.
- Remind the group about the material they should complete at home before your next meeting.
- Briefly reinforce or review the session's main points.
- Preview the next session; mention the primary topic at least.
- End in prayer. (For prayer helps, see "Lead in prayer," p. 171.)

Session 2: Who Is God?

1. Introductory discussion.
- Attention-getter: Display a photograph, work of art, a decorated baked good or play a brief musical selection. Ask the group what they can tell you about the artist, chef, or musician based on his or her creation. Now ask the group what materials or tools the person had to use to create the piece.
- Read the definition for the word *created* found in Genesis 1:1.
- Ask: How is this different from the way we normally use the word? What does the meaning of this word in Genesis teach us about God?

2. Review the three foundational concepts from session 1.

3. Ask the group to share what they learned from Psalm 119 in the "Find Out More" section.

4. Explore God's creation.
- On a board, write the numbers 1 to 6 vertically.

- Read through Genesis 1:1 to 2:3. Stop at the end of each day of creation and ask the group to identify what God created on that day. Write those things on the board.
- The Hebrew word translated as "light" in verse 3 is different from the word translated as "light" in verse 14. The Hebrew word *or*, found in verse 3, is light in general and is often used symbolically of God and life. *Maor*, found in verse 14, is more specifically a luminous body, such as a lamp. (See *The Complete Word Study Old Testament* for more on these words.)

5. Ask and discuss: What does the order and scope of creation teach us about God?

6. Discuss God's right and authority.
- Read Psalm 24:1–2. Ask the group what claim God makes. Is His claim a fair one? Why or why not?
- Use a board or large sheet of paper to draw a table. Label one column "Rights" and the other "Responsibilities." Ask the class to name things they own, like a car, home, or pet. Under each column list applicable rights and responsibilities for the items named.
- Ask: How do you think God should exercise His rights and responsibilities of ownership over your life?

7. Jesus and Creation
- Read Colossians 1:15–17 and ask the group what it teaches about Jesus.
- Read Matthew 28:18. Ask how this truth impacts Jesus's claims in John 14:6.

Session 3: Why Am I Here?

1. Review the main points from session 2 and "Find Out More."

2. Opening object lesson—Show a photo and discuss how it is *like* and *unlike* the actual subject.

3. Discuss: God created us in His image.
   * Read Genesis 1:26–28; 2:7–9, 15–25.
   * Discuss the meaning of the word *image* as described on page 39.
   * Ask: What qualities are found in humans that do not exist in the rest of creation?
   * Ask: How are humans *like* God? How are we *not* like God?

4. Discuss God's purpose for us.
   * Read Ecclesiastes 1:2, 14, 16–17; 2:10–11; and 12:13.
   * Ask: Why did Solomon not find fulfillment in his quest for knowledge and riches?
   * Read Colossians 1:16; Isaiah 43:7; and Acts 17:24–28.
   * Ask: What do these passages teach about our purpose in life?
   * Read Romans 8:29.
   * Ask: What additional truth does it teach about God's purpose for us?

(Caution: Steer clear of discussing predestination versus free will. If needed, refer back to the comments in the session on Romans 8:29.)

Session 4: What Went Wrong?

1. Review the main points from session 3 and ask the group what they learned about Jesus from "Find Out More."

2. Play a quick game of darts to demonstrate the meaning of sin. Divide four volunteers into two teams. Just keep a simple score by adding the total for each team. You may want to have a small prize for the winners. Chances are none of your volunteers will hit the bull's-eye. Use the darts to demonstrate the definition for sin as explained on page 51. It doesn't matter if one person barely missed the center and another hit the wall—they both "sinned," or missed the target.

3. Read Romans 3:23. Discuss how sin is anything less than the perfect image of God. Ask for some examples of sin. Based on the definition you've discussed, ask your group if they've ever sinned.

4. Define and discuss the first sin.
  - Read Genesis 2:15–17.
  - Ask: Why would God impose restrictions on Adam and Eve?
  - Read Genesis 3:1–8. Review "Satan" sidebar if needed.
  - Ask: What specific doubts do you think Satan planted in Eve's mind about God? Why do you think Eve chose to disobey God? Why did Adam?

5. All sin has consequences.
  - Turn to Genesis 3:9–24.
  - Ask: How did God immediately respond to Adam and Eve's sin?
  - Work with the group to identify all the consequences of sin from the passage.
  - Read Romans 6:23. Use it to emphasize the ultimate consequence of sin.
  - Discuss the significance of "spiritual death."

6. Read Hebrews 4:14–15. Ask the group what it teaches about Jesus and how this can help us in our daily lives.

Session 5: How Did God Respond?

1. Review the main points from session 4 and ask the group what they learned about sin and its effects from "Find Out More."

2. Opening discussion—Ask the group about their Christmas traditions. Ask: What first comes to your mind when you think about Christmas?

3. Read Luke 19:10. (Note: *Son of man* was a term Jesus often used to refer to Himself.)

4. Ask: Why did Jesus come? Does this fact give new meaning to the birth of Jesus?

5. Read Matthew 1:18–25. Say: Name all the facts you can from the passage about the baby to be born, including the significance of His names.

6. The birth of Jesus
   - Ask: What would you expect the birth of someone as important as the Son of God to be like?
   - Read Luke 2:6–7.
   - Ask: Use your imagination to think about the birth of Jesus in a stable where animals were kept. Describe what His birth must have been like.

7. The birth announcement
   - Ask: What is the most elaborate birth announcement you've ever seen?
   - Direct the group to turn to Luke 2:8–20. Ask for a volunteer to describe this heavenly birth announcement.
   - Ask: What else do we learn about Jesus from the additional names of Jesus that the angels tell to the shepherds?

8. Heaven's perspective
   - Refer to Colossians 2:9 and John 1:1–4, 14. Briefly discuss the nature of Jesus. (Other Scriptures supporting the deity of Jesus include: Colossians 1:15–17; John 20:28; 1 Timothy 1:15–17; and Hebrews 1:3.)
   - Read Philippians 2:5–11 while the group views photos of earth from space. Discuss the questions on page 64. If you have access to the Internet, downloads images to show.

9. Preview the coming week's session. Closing comment: "You will see that religion *does not* mend the broken relationship with God."

Session 6: How Can I Be Saved?

1. Review the main points from session 5 and ask the group what they learned about Jesus and themselves through the analogy of a shepherd and his sheep as described in "Find Out More."

2. Opening discussion—Ask the group to define *religion*. Ask what ideas people have about what it takes to become or be a Christian.

3. Read John 3:1–2 about Nicodemus.
   - Based on the passage and the explanation in the study, ask your group to describe Nicodemus. (You may need to help explain about the Pharisees and the Sanhedrin.)
   - Ask: Do you know religious people like Nicodemus today? What did Nicodemus believe about Jesus?

4. Read John 3:3–8 about being "born again."
   - Ask: Based on Nicodemus's comments and Jesus's reply, what do you think was going through Nicodemus's mind?
   - Ask: What does it mean to be a part of the kingdom of God? What *is* the kingdom of God? What did Jesus say must happen for a person to be a part of God's kingdom?
   - Ask: Who is willing to take a stab at explaining "born again?" (Be ready to explain if no one answers or to gently supplement someone's answer.)

5. The effects of the Spirit
   - Ask for several members of the group to tell about effects of wind they have seen.
   - Ask: How are the wind and the Holy Spirit similar? What do you think are some of the effects of the working of the Holy Spirit? Have you witnessed any of these? Experienced any of these?

6. Belief—an active trust
   - Read John 3:9–15.
   - Explain the meaning of Jesus "being lifted up."
   - Read John 3:16–18.
   - Say: Jesus's purpose in coming to earth was to save, not condemn. Everyone is already condemned because of sin. But by believing in Jesus we can be saved.

- Demonstrate the meaning of *belief*. Put a chair in the middle of the group. Ask if they "believe" the chair can support them. Now ask who will demonstrate faith in the chair by sitting down. Similarly, our belief in Jesus has to be more than lip service. It must be an active faith that causes us to put our lives in His hands.

7. Before and after
   - Find a dramatic before-and-after photo to show to your group.
   - Read Titus 3:3–7 and ask the group to describe the spiritual before-and-after seen in these verses.
   - Ask this rhetorical question: "Are you a 'before' or an 'after'?"

Session 7: How High Is the Price?

1. Opening discussion
   - The title of the movie and book *Dead Man Walking* is based on the traditional call of "Dead man walking, dead man walking here!" made by a prison guard as a condemned prisoner is led onto death row for the first time.
   - Ask: What does this have to do with what we've been talking about in these last sessions? How are we — or how have we been — like "dead men (women) walking?"

2. Review
   - Review the main points from session 6 and ask the group what they learned about God's dealings with sinful people from "Find Out More."
   - Say: In today's session we will see Jesus's willingness to pay the penalty *our* sins have earned.

3. Read or talk through the account of Jesus's arrest in Matthew 26:47–56.
   - Ask for a volunteer to describe the scene in the garden in her own words.

- Ask: What evidence do we find in this passage that shows Jesus willingly submitted to arrest?

4. Read Mark 14:53–65 about the Jewish trial.
   - Ask: Why do you think Jesus defended, or didn't defend, Himself the way He did?
   - Ask: What evidence got Jesus convicted by the Jewish leaders?

5. Trial before Pilate
   - Briefly explain who Pilate was and why Jesus had to appear before him.
   - Recount the events in John 18:28–40 and ask: How did Jesus describe the nature of His kingship?
   - Read John 19:1–11 and ask: What evidence do you see here that the death of Jesus was God's plan all along?
   - Read John 19:12–16.

6. Jesus's obedience to the Father's plan
   - Read John 10:14–18. Say: Jesus said this well before His arrest, trial, and death.
   - Ask: How does this teaching of Jesus show His knowledge of the Father's plan and His willingness to obey it?
   - Ask: What will the Shepherd do to protect His sheep? Who has the authority to take the Shepherd's (Jesus's) life?

7. Conclusion—Read Matthew 20:28. Ask: How does Jesus' statement once again reveal His purpose in coming to earth? How does it fit in with today's session?

Session 8: Isn't This Too Good to Be True?

1. Review the main points from session 7 and ask the group what they learned from Isaiah 53 in "Find Out More."

2. Opening discussion
   - Ask: What's the biggest sacrifice you ever saw an individual make for someone else? What did it cost her?

What is the biggest sacrifice *you* ever made for someone else? What did it cost you?
- Read Romans 5:6–8 and ask: What did Jesus sacrifice for us? What were we like when He made the sacrifice?

3. Explore the various responses to Jesus and His death found in Luke 23:26–56 using the questions on page 96. Ask: Why do you think people respond in various ways to Jesus today?

4. What did Jesus's death accomplish?
- Object lesson: Offer to make a trade with someone in the group. You will need to trade something good in return for something bad or worthless. For instance, you could offer to give someone a dollar in trade for pocket lint.
- Read Romans 3:21–25 from the NLT version printed on page 96.
- Also read 2 Corinthians 5:21.
- Ask: Describe this great exchange that God offers to us. According to what you've learned so far in this study, why did Jesus have to die? What did His death accomplish?

5. Read Luke 24:1–12 about Jesus's resurrection. Ask: Why do you think the disciples did not believe the women's story? Would you?

Session 9: Is There Hope for My Future?

1. Review the main points of the last session—particularly what the death of Christ accomplished. Ask: What have you learned about the nature of Jesus from "Find Out More"?

2. Opening discussion
Have you ever received news that seemed too good to be true? Maybe it was so wonderful and perhaps even unlikely you had a hard time believing it. What finally convinced you?

3. Proof of the Resurrection
- Read Luke 24:36–49. Ask: What physical evidence does Jesus give the disciples to convince them He is alive?
- Read 1 Corinthians 15:3–8. Ask: How many appearances of Jesus are recorded here? If you heard these people for yourself would it convince you?
- Have the group turn to the inset on page 107 entitled "Martyrs for Jesus."
- Ask: Does this evidence impress you at all? If so, in what way?

4. The importance of the Resurrection for us today
- Ask: What are some of the different ideas people have about life after death?
- Read 1 Thessalonians 4:13–18 and Philippians 3:20–21. (There is no need to get into the different views of the end times. Focus on the fact that Jesus will return and that His victory over death makes our resurrection possible.)
- Ask: What does Jesus's resurrection make possible for us? (The Resurrection is proof that everything Jesus said and did is true. It confirms He is God and that salvation is through Him and is found in no one else.)

5. Bringing it all together
- Everything during this study has led up to this point. Some of your members may be ready to make a decision about Jesus. Make sure you leave plenty of time for this section. Be in prayer specifically for this moment, before and during your study.
- Go through the study summary points under "What Does It All Mean?" on page 109. Clarify as you feel the need and answer questions as they arise.
- Turn to the "How Should I Respond?" section on page 110. Help your group understand how to respond to Jesus and His invitation for salvation through a relationship with Him. Encourage them to think about how they should respond to Jesus. Offer to talk to them outside of your group time.

- Tell the group that the next three sessions will show them some of the basics of following Jesus.

Session 10: What Now?

1. Opening discussion
Read 2 Corinthians 5:17. Ask: Have you ever wished you could have a "do over" in life? Have you ever wanted to wipe the slate clean and start fresh?

2. Ask your group what they learned from Romans 6:1–14 about the nature of a Christian's new life in Christ in "Find Out More."

3. Read Acts 1:1–11 about Jesus's last days on earth.
   - Ask: Describe Jesus's 40 days on earth between His resurrection and ascension.
   - Ask: What specific instructions did Jesus give His followers?
   - Ask: Who would help them carry out these instructions?

4. Read Acts 2:1–4 about the arrival of the Holy Spirit.
   - Ask: What do you remember about the Holy Spirit— who He is and what He does in the lives of believers— from last week's session?
   - Briefly discuss the points in the inset, "Understanding the Holy Spirit," from session 9 on page 105.
   - Ask: How could the Holy Spirit help Jesus's followers carry out His instructions? How can the Holy Spirit help you to follow Jesus?

5. Read Acts 2:36–47 about the first Christians. Ask: What was the very first thing these new Christians did? To what four things were the Christians devoted (v. 42)?

6. Sharing from the group—Be prepared to share your own examples for one or more of the following if no one speaks up.

- Ask: Will someone share about the place God's Word, the Bible, has in your life? It may even be a recent development.
- Ask: Have you ever experienced *koinonia* (fellowship, intimacy, and sharing among a group of believers) as described in this passage? If so, how?
- Ask: What significance does the Lord's Supper have for you?
- Ask: What place does prayer have in your life?

7. Read 1 Corinthians 12:12–18, 25–27 about the church. Ask: What does this analogy teach about a church and what it should be? According to this passage, what place should church have in the life of a believer? Is church optional?

8. Conclusion
- Ask: What did you learn this week about the first Christians that surprised you the most? Is there anything about the way they lived the Christian life you think would be difficult for you today? If so, why?

Session 11: How Do I Get to Know God?

1. Ask the group what they learned about baptism in "Find Out More."

2. Interest-generating activity—Ask your group to pretend they've been hired as a stand-in for their favorite singer or actor for various public appearances. Ask who they would choose to "be" and how they would have to prepare to be successful.

3. God's purpose for us
- Read Romans 8:29 from the New Living Translation (NLT): *"For God knew his people in advance, and he chose them to become like his Son."*
- Ask: Why do you think God wants us to be like Jesus? How do we become more like Jesus?
- Read 2 Corinthians 5:16–21 to help with your answer.

(Note: As we become more like Jesus we reflect the glory of God to a lost world. Remember, God created us to bring glory to Himself. The more we become like Jesus, the more we fulfill God's purpose for us.)

- Ask: What does the story about Moses in 2 Corinthians 3 teach us about a Christian's relationship with God?
- Ask: What is the Holy Spirit's role in you becoming like Jesus? (Read 2 Corinthians 3:18 to help with your answer.)

4. Spending time with God

- Ask: How do get to know another person? What do you have to do to develop a deep and trusting friendship?
- Discuss how growing a relationship with God is similar.
- Ask: Based on what you learned in this session, how would you define *prayer*? Describe Jesus's prayer life. Describe the type of prayer life that pleases God. Were you surprised by anything you learned about prayer?
- Ask your group to turn to the sidebar entitled "How to Have a Quiet Time" on page 133. Walk them through these suggestions and share from your own experience.
- Ask: Did anyone use the information in this week's session to have a quiet time or to spend time with God? How did it go?

Session 12: How Do I Follow God?

1. Review "Find Out More." Ask the group if they were surprised by the promises about prayer.

2. Object Lesson—Ask two volunteers to participate. Create a mini-obstacle course in your meeting room by arranging several items such as a chair, stool, or table. One volunteer is to verbally instruct a blindfolded volunteer through the obstacle course. If the "sighted" volunteer does his or her job effectively, the "blind" volunteer will have the information needed to navigate the course one obstacle at a time and come out the other side. The rest of the

group can also instruct the "blind" volunteer, but their directions don't have to be correct. Advise the blind volunteer to tune out the other group members and listen only to the guide. The guide is the one who will always give them the right directions.

After the activity, ask the group how this illustrates the way God speaks to us through the Holy Spirit.

3. Actively following the Holy Spirit
- Ask: Why should Christians follow the Holy Spirit? (Note: See 1 Corinthians 6:19–20 and Romans 8:5–12. Make sure the discussion that follows this question includes the truths that: Christians belong to God; Christians have the Holy Spirit living inside; and a life following the Spirit pleases God and fills a Christian with joy.)
- Read 1 Corinthians 2:11–14 and ask: If you have recently become a Christian, how are you experiencing the presence of the Holy Spirit? Do you have a new understanding of spiritual things? Have you wondered why your non-Christian friends or relatives don't "get" it?
- For an example read Acts 16:6–10 and ask: How was Paul sensitive to the Holy Spirit's leading? How did he adjust his actions to God's direction?
- Ask: What are some ways the Spirit can guide us? (Note: Be sure and share with the class that visions are not a primary, or even a common, way the Spirit speaks to Christians. Stress things like Bible reading, prayer, and the counsel of godly men and women.)

4. Read Galatians 5:16–25 about the work of the Holy Spirit. If you have access to a board, re-create the table on page 142 of this book. List the characteristics on both sides of the table as the group names them. Be sure to emphasize the fact that these changes don't take place overnight. It takes time for God to shape us and it is only possible through our yielded obedience to the Holy Spirit.

5. Failing to follow
- Ask: Raise your hand if you are always completely obedient to God and never choose your own way. (You shouldn't have any hands raised!)
- Say: All Christians still sin. Hopefully, we will sin less next year than we do this year because we are allowing God to shape us. But what should we do when we choose to sin?
- Read James 4:1–10. Ask: Name some of the sinful actions and attitudes James points out in the lives of his readers. How does James challenge them to respond?
- Say: Whether our sin is gossip or selfishness or murder or theft, God calls us to humble repentance before Him. This cannot be cursory repentance. It must be genuine.
- Ask: According to James 4:7–9, what does repentance look like?
- Ask: What does God promise to do when we confess our sins and repent? (See James 4:10 and 1 John 1:9.)

6. Conclusion—Since this is the last session for your group, be sure to leave plenty of time at the end for the following.
- Ask: Are there any questions or comments about anything we have covered in the last 12 weeks?
- Ask: Would anyone be willing to share what God has done in their life through the course of this study?

New Hope® Publishers is a division of WMU®, an international organization that challenges Christian believers to understand and be radically involved in God's mission. For more information about WMU, go to www.wmu.com. More information about New Hope books may be found at www.newhopepublishers.com. New Hope books may be purchased at your local bookstore.

If you've been blessed by this book, we would like to hear your story. The publisher and author welcome your comments and suggestions at: newhopereader@wmu.org.

Other Discipleship Resources from

New Hope

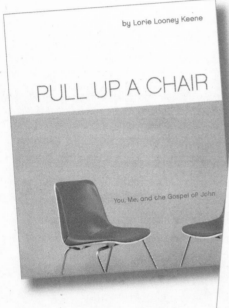

<table>
<tr><td>Pull Up a Chair</td><td>Set Apart</td></tr>
<tr><td>You, Me, and the Gospel of John</td><td>A 6-Week Study of the Beatitudes</td></tr>
<tr><td>Lorie Looney Keene</td><td>Jennifer Kennedy Dean</td></tr>
<tr><td>ISBN-10: 1-59669-202-2</td><td>ISBN-10: 1-59669-263-4</td></tr>
<tr><td>ISBN-13: 978-1-59669-202-2</td><td>ISBN-13: 978-1-59669-263-3</td></tr>
</table>